One Day at a Time, Lord

A Uniquely *Homespun* Daily Devotional

Rae Snowden Martin

New Harbor Press

RAPID CITY, SD

Martin/New Harbor Press
1601 Mt. Rushmore Rd, Ste 3288
Rapid City, SD 57701
www.newharborpress.com

One Day at a Time, Lord / Rae Snowden Martin. -- 1st ed.
ISBN 978-1-63357-334-5

Cover photo by Billy Martin

Acknowledgements

My mother, Rae Snowden Martin and I first acknowledge God for all things.

For the original printing in 2002, my mother acknowledged a neighbor in her senior park, Joyce Middleton, for typesetting clippings that could not be read well. I am certain that without her help this would not have gotten printed. I would love to have someone in her family find a copy.

Mom also acknowledged me, Billy Martin, her eldest son. Her expectations were higher than what I did, but whatever they were, they were too high for what I was capable of at that time. What's important in the acknowledgements was that she gave all donations, all proceeds, to *First Christian Church (Disciples of Christ)* - in Venice Beach, Florida.

In keeping with supporting the church, I plan to donate 10% of all the sales from this book to my church, *Godspeak Calvary Chapel*, in Newbury Park, California *(gccto.com)*. Pastor Rob McCoy is the single most-important person in my Christian journey. My first realization that God was guiding my life came in 2012 on my tenth sobriety date in AA. I had begun building a Christian life but never testified to it. In fact, Rob McCoy baptized me a few weeks before this book went into publication.

My Christian roots were my parents, who both, quietly, meditatively, prayed every morning and night and I imagine a lot of other times, too. My mom taught us, the "Now I lay me down to sleep," prayer. My sister told me not long ago that she thought it was an awful prayer. It scared her before going to bed thinking she may not wake up.

The Community Church of East Williston on Long Island, NY, was our family church. I got baptized as an infant and confirmed in middle school. Mom was very proud of our family participation in the church. We were rewarded with candy bars as grade-schoolers. The purpose of religion all came together for me as I was coming of age in Young People's with Mr. Frietag.

After high school, there was no Christianity in my life until I went to AA in 2002. If there had been a cross above the door, I would not have gone in. However, as many of us say and do believe God brought me to AA and AA brought me to God.

At work, in my last job, I had another person work on my Christian thinking. His name is Mark Horowitz. I found it most fascinating to learn about Jesus from a Jew. I see a clear path and the Jews were certainly part of the Christian Journey. Mark has a regular e-mail column with the same name as his first book, *Nuggets of Wisdom*.

Finally, for the past few years I have had the opportunity to belong to my first Bible Study. I was clearly the least educated about the Bible. I was drawn to the realization that every principle I found in AA was consistent with the Bible. However, it was the Christian fellowship delving into our studies that had the most impact on me.

I got down to work on re-finishing this book, *One Day at a Time, Lord*. As a result, I have decided to put together a daily devotional of my own. It will be just like this with gleanings of Christian and AA meditations together as one message. It is titled, *GOD (as we understand Him)*.

I have made the acknowledgements a lot about me I suppose since I embarked on the long process of getting this published. All I have done really is act as a typesetter, bit writer, partial editor, proof-reader, and in the end a project manager.

There is no author. My mom wrote nothing of her own. She simply collected clippings and word phrases she heard over her 88 years. Not one inclusion can be much less than 25 years old.

A great many came from her constant companion, *Guideposts*. All I've done is taken my mom's book to a point where readers can find it easily.

I am fully cognizant that the real purpose of the entire endeavor is to spread the Word. The ultimate accomplishment is finding readers like you. So, for everyone who discovers a copy of this book, my mother thanks and acknowledges all of you, too.

Dedication

This book is dedicated to my mother. It was her life's work.

I don't know how many years of "gleanings" this represents. Nor even when my mom started editing them or gluing them onto pages with dates. I knew a lot about the printing process and had she told me what she was doing, I would have set her on her way, out of the gates, with margins and gaps in the centerfold. Ironically, had she done that, that probably would have been the end of the book story, completed in 2002 for her eightieth birthday.

I remember the time especially in my life. I had no God and was battling alcoholism. I was in no shape to do much of a better job than I did. I basically made photocopies and stapled a yellow cover on them. It would have taken a great deal of work, I figured, to re-paste all of the pages. I wanted it to be done so I could say I did it, and make up for all of the years of my life I wasted and as payback for the ways I had treated my mother.

My last day of drinking was the day I drove my mother to the airport after a family reunion and celebration for her birthday in Las Vegas. I'll never forget what she said to me about my drinking then, something I never heard in AA, "You can lick this thing." It gave me real hope.

In lieu of that, in 12-step programs, we first admit we can't lick this thing on our own. We need God's help. We also discover a fellowship sharing their experience, strength and hope. I haven't had to drink since. Reading my copy of her book, right there staring daily at me, was my minimal effort on a beautiful book edited by my mom.

Once I even heard her reference to them as the "bunged-up" copies. However, her saddest lament was not understanding why more people weren't flocking to read it. She knew nothing of publishing a book. She took the lack of word-of-mouth personally, like we all do.

I never promised to her that I would do a proper job some-day. As my faith grew, from little in 2002 to today, eighteen years later, I realized that my mother was a direct conduit to God for me. I had a calling to not only fix the botched job, but more importantly, feel that I had done as much as I could to help her reach more readers for her collection of inspired words. I dedicated myself to my mother's mission of reaching more people by giving everyone access to it online. This is the result.

January

Lord, whatever you have in store for me is alright.
You've got my address and I've got Yours.

NOTE: * indicates Rae's rating system

Jan 1

I pray that God will guide me
one day at a time in the new year.
I pray that for each day,
God will supply the wisdom
and the strength that I need. Amen.

A Prayer for the Year That is Here

God of the years that lie behind us,
Lord of the years that stretch before,
Weaver of all ties that bind us,
Keeper and King of the open door:
Grant us hope and courage glowing
White and pure as the stars above;
Grant us faith as full stream flowing,
From the heights of Your eternal love.
Out of the ruins of doubt and sorrow,
Out of the aches and pains and tears,
Help us to fashion a new tomorrow,
Free from the anguish of blighting fears.
All through the seasons of flowing and reaping,
All through the harvest of song and tears,
Hold us close in Your tender keeping.
O Maker of all New Years!

Jan 2

Dear Lord, clear my mind as I kneel before you,
Help me to seek you in all that I do.
Help me to know where you are leading me today,
Help me to follow each step of the way.
I pray not for riches or worldly fame,
I just ask for the strength to lift up Your name.
If a friend has a need or a burden to bear,
Help me be there to show that I care.
Help me to be all You want me to be,
Let others see Jesus living in me.
Then when the day has ended and sleep takes control,
Dear Lord, let them say, "It is well with my soul."

Jan 3

Refusing to ask for help when you need it,
is refusing someone the chance to be helpful.

# # #

Lord, please make my prayers as constant as Your love.

Jan 4

O, God, my Maker from whom I hold my life in trust,
give me this day the grace I may need to stand for Thee openly,
serve Thee faithfully and follow Thee fearlessly.

#

Though we know not what the future holds,
we know the One who holds the future.

Jan 5

Filled with God's Love

No half measures, please! urges Canon R.C. Stephens: as Christians, we should open our hearts and souls to God, not hold back from him.

Some of us pride ourselves that we can suppress our emotions and show a stiff upper lip in times of crisis, yet even the most stoical of us cannot contain ourselves, times when the flood-gates burst and our hearts overflow.

The idea of men and women as receptacles holding spiritual things to pass on to others is found several times in the New Testament. St. Paul was a "chosen vessel" for God, but he remained empty until Ananias had laid his hands on him that he might receive his sight and be filled with the Holy Ghost (*Acts 9: 15-17*).

Characteristically, St. Paul used it to describe fellow Christians (*2 Timothy 2:20-21*). He pointed out that there are many kinds of vessels, some of silver and gold, others of earthenware, and the material of which they are made does not alter their usefulness. Just so are there many people, some gifted, others quite ordinary, whose differences do not change the fact that each is essential to God's purpose.

But the metaphor does not stop there. A container is often only partly full, but the Scriptures do not mention partial measures, for they are concerned only with fullness. Christ's disciples are to be "full of goodness, filled with knowledge," (*Romans 15:14*) full of faith, mercy, and joy. St. Paul had to be filled with the Holy Spirit and then his love and enthusiasm bubbled over and changed his life.

Men and Women are God's chosen vessels, but they are of little use if they are only half-full. When we pour a cup of tea, we are careful not to fill it up to the brim, so that it doesn't spill over, and this is what we tend to do in our lives; we are careful not to be too Christian. But a life only partly filled with the love of Christ can never overflow onto the lives of others.

Jan 6

For Our Children

Lord, look kindly on our children,
fashioned by You from the womb.
Keep fear and trouble far from them,
and when life's storms come,
guide our children to safety.
In days to come – Give them faith, hope and love,
and keep them always by your side. Amen

Jan 7

Prayer for the New Year

O God, our heavenly Father, as we enter
upon this new year, we commit ourselves to Thy
faithful care and keeping. Give us the grace so
to love Thee with all our heart and soul and
mind and strength that we may live without fear,
and so to love our neighbors as ourselves that
we may live without reproach. As our days so let
our strength be; and grant that no chance or
change may turn us aside for the doing of Thy
holy will, through Jesus Christ our Lord.
Amen

Jan 8

While faith makes all things possible,
It is love that makes all things easy.

#

The light of God surrounds me,
The love of God enfolds me,
The power of God protects me,
the presence of God watches over me,
wherever I am, God is!
(From *Guideposts Outreach Ministries*)

Jan 9

Lord, give me the courage to be true
To You in all I say and do,
Give me your love to keep me sweet
To everyone I chance to meet.
Give me Your power to keep me strong.
Grant me your presence all day long.
Give me the faith that all may see
How very real You are to me.
Give me the wisdom to choose the best.
Help me perform each task with zest.
Give me the vision to see Your plan.
Use me, Lord, wherever You can.

Jan 10

My Daily Prayer

Dear God, as I begin this day
Let me turn my thoughts to You,
And ask Your help in guiding me
In everything I say and do.
Give me the patience that I need
To keep my peace of mind.
And with life's cares, I hope, Dear God,
Some happiness to find.
Let me live but for today,
Not worrying what's ahead.
For I have trust that You will see
I get my "Daily Bread."

Jan 11

Serenity Prayer

O God, give us the courage
to accept with serenity
the things we cannot change.
Give us the courage to change
the things that should be changed.
And give us the wisdom to
distinguish the one from the other.

Jan 12

My Prayer

Give me wisdom, Lord I pray,
That as I read your Word each day,
The message I must need to know –
That in your Spirit I can grow.

Give me strength, dear Lord, I pray,
Strength to follow in your way.
And in this world of sin and shame,
I'll gladly stand to praise your name.

Give me faith dear Lord, I pray,
To know as I go forth each day,
You give to me with love divine,
Your promises to claim as mine.
Gladys Naphas

Jan 13

The Gift

If I can make it through the day,
The sun will shine much brighter.
And all the burdens I must bear.
Will be a little lighter.

There'll be joy in my heart,
And friendship with each giving,
I'll bow my head in silent prayer,
And thank God that I'm living.

Frank Stokowski

Jan 14

Trust Him, when thy darkest thoughts assail thee,
Trust Him when thy faith is small,
Trust Him, when to simply trust Him, is the hardest thing of all.

Rosalind Russell

Jan 15

God's Will

I know not by what methods rare,
But, this I know: God answers prayer.
I know not if the blessing sought,
Will come in just the guise I thought.
I leave my prayer to him alone,
Whose will is wiser than my own.
Eliza M. Hickok

Jan 16

Bountiful Blessing

May the greatest of gifts come and linger
With us as and our loved ones today,
To bring us sunshine of gladness
And banish all sadness away.
To guard the ways of the future,
To light all the paths we have trod;
For the greatest of gifts and of treasures,
Is the bountiful blessing of God.
Brian O'Higgins

Jan 17 *

Faith is the Key to Heaven

Oh, Father, grant once more to men
A simple, childlike Faith again,
Forgetting color, race and creed
And seeing only the heart's deep need.
For faith alone can save man's soul
And lead him to a higher goal.
For there's but one unfailing course,
We win by Faith and not by force.
Helen Steiner Rice

Jan 18

Minds are like parachutes
They only work when they are open

###

Heavenly Father, grant me the wisdom, patience and strength
to cope with today's concerns. And when tomorrow comes, I'll
be back to ask again! Amen
Doris L. Mueller

Jan 19

The Meaning of Perfection

God does not expect us to be perfect in ourselves, says Canon R.C. Stephens, but requires us to strive to fulfil His purpose.

Sermons as a rule are not popular; one however, still retains its popularity, and that is "The Sermon on The Mount" (*Matthew 5-7*), which Jesus preached to his friends – and this includes you and me. It tells us how the citizens of His kingdom should behave, and ends with a story of those who obey and those who, on the other hand, reject his 'sayings.'

The most disconcerting verse in this discourse comes in the middle: "Be ye therefore perfect" (*Matthew 5:48*) as your heavenly Father is. How can any one of us be perfect? No one is absolutely good. But, Jesus would not have said this if it was impossible. The difficulty arises over the interpretation of the word 'perfect'. We generally assume it means "absolute goodness, absence of wrong," but in Scripture it is the translation of a word which means "an end , fulfilled, complete, mature."

Christ did not exhort us to reach a certain standard of goodness but to strive to fulfil God's purpose for us. The sermon urges us to pray, to love others, to be forgiving and not to trust in material things, and this will eventually bring us to God, which is the end for which he created us.

Perfection, rightly understood, is not an impractical idea for the Christian, but it is the carrying out of God's purpose, which will be achieved with Christ's help if we are faithful to His teaching. The way will be different for each of us, and we shall not reap instant rewards. It is a long journey, but we have all eternity before us. "Let us advance toward maturity" – perfection (*Hebrews 6: 2*).

Jan 20

Beautiful Savior,
My friend and my guide,
There's peace in my heart
Because You're at my side.
Good Shepherd,
Who cares for me,
Light of my soul,
Wise teacher and healer,
Your love makes me whole.

Jan 21

We cannot direct the wind,
but we can adjust the sails.

###

Lord, whatever you have in store for me is alright.
You've got my address and I've got Yours.

Jan 22

When I get discouraged
and want to give up,
remind me Lord,
that winners don't quit
and quitters don't win.

Jan 23

Lord, grant me a quiet mind,
that trusting Thee,
for Thou art kind,
I may go on without a fear,
for thou my Lord,
art always near.

Jan 24

He who guides the swallows flight,
Keep me safe through day and night,
He who guides the sea and land,
Take me safely by the hand.
He who guides the stars at night,
Teach my eyes to see Thee bright,
He who guides the soul its way,
Teach me faithfully to pray."
Elsie C. Offner

Jan 25

As I Prepare to Meet the Day

Let the dawn fall softly
On my shoulders, Lord,
As I prepare to meet the day.
Let the sunshine wrap its warmth 'round me

As I go along my way.
Let me feel Your presence near me,
As the gentle breezes play
Through blades of grass, and in the trees,
Causing leaves to sway.
Let me show some kindness
To each person that I meet,
Let me see Your image
In each person that I greet,
Joyceln Zaiontz

Jan 26

Almighty, most Holy, most high God,
Thank You for paying attention to small things.
Thank You for valuing the insignificant.
Thank You for being in the lilies of the field
And the birds of the air.
Thank You for caring about me. Amen
Richard Foster

Jan 27

GOD HEALS

For each and every aching heart
In this old world today,
There is a cure – one safe and sure:
Just this, learn how to pray.
Pour out your aching heart to Him
Who understands and cares;
He's the only one who knows.
The only one who shares.
God can – and does – heal broken hearts,
And gives us life anew;
He's ready – waiting – for your prayers;
He'll do it now – for you.

Jan 28

No Thought of Reward

At the Last Judgement, we shall be known by the practical help we have given to others, explains Canon R.C. Stephens.

The Devotional Life of our Lord is evident from His emphasis on prayer, His knowledge and love for the Scriptures and His weekly visit to the synagogue, and most Christians base their lives on the same foundations.

It comes therefore as a shock to find that in His picture of the Last Judgement (*Matthew 25: 31-46*), none of these are mentioned. The separation of people into sheep and goats is determined, not by spiritual obligations carried out, but by the practical test of administering to those in trouble – the hungry and the thirsty, those without clothes, the homeless, the sick and even those in prison.

Two principles for doing this were given. First, there was to be no discrimination between those who had fallen on hard times through no fault of their own, and those who had only themselves to blame – need alone was to be considered; and, secondly, only disinterested service without any thought of reward would be acceptable as done to the King Himself.

If helping those in need impartially is the yardstick by which we shall be judged, are prayers, Bible reading and public worship of any importance? Of course they are, for they can deepen our love for God and we have our Lord's example to follow; but these can never take the place of compassion and practical help, for to perform religious duties expecting to gain something would completely destroy their purpose, and become hypocrisy.

The prophets made this quite clear when they denounced those who, although orthodox in religious observance, neglected the oppressed, the fatherless and widows (*Isaiah 1 15-17*). If our devotions do not result in helping our neighbors, they count for nothing in the sight of God.

Jan 29 *

Thank God For Little Things

Thank you, God, for little things
That often come our way –
The things we take for granted
But don't mention when we pray –

The unexpected courtesy,
The thoughtful kindly deed –
A hand reached out to help us
In the time of sudden need –
Oh, make us more aware, dear God,
Of little daily graces
That come to us with "sweet surprise"
From never- dreamed-of places.
Helen Steiner Rice

Jan 30

A plea for serenity

God, mold my spirit whole again,
And grant me peace of mind.
Please calm my secret doubts and fears.
The courage I will find,
To face ever-changing tide –
Darkest night or dreary day,
Knowing that you're guiding me,
Always near me, lest I stray.
Gorda Jeffcoat

Jan 31 **

God Grant Me
Courage and Hope
For every day,
Faith to guide me
Along my way,
Understanding
And Wisdom, too,
And Grace to Accept
What life gives me to do.
Helen Steiner Rice

February

We can never fall below the reach of God's love.

Feb 1

Tools of the Trade

We often underestimate our ability to assist God in His work, says Canon R.C. Stephens

Tools fascinate me – I love looking at them and I could spend hours in an ironmonger's shop. This could indicate that I am excellent at woodwork but while I like to make things, I am no expert. I take great care in my measurements and angles but the finished article never looks right and is a bit of a bodged-up job. On the other hand, friends who seem to take far less trouble turn out a professional piece of work.

Jesus was a carpenter and I wonder what His work was like? I think of Him working in His shop with what must have been crude tools compared with those of today. Nevertheless, I am sure His work was excellent. The yokes for the animals would fit snugly and wouldn't cause them to suffer, and the cradles would have no splinters to get into tiny fingers.

But the time came for Him to leave the shop to do work of a different sort – human instruments for the spreading of His message. He chose twelve whom he called apostles (*Matthew 10:2*) and we find it difficult to understand why He chose these particular men. Matthew had betrayed his nation by becoming a collector of taxes for the Romans in order to make money. Peter was a coward and a liar, there was Judas and some were so insignificant that we know almost nothing about them except their names, and every one of them forsook Him in His hour of need. Yet these were the men He chose to be His partners and the Acts of the Apostles and the spread of the Gospel show He was justified in His choice, and how He achieved His purpose with the most unlikely of people.

He is still looking for human instruments for His work and many appeals are made for volunteers, but the immediate response of many is, "Oh, I couldn't do that," or, "I'm not good enough," and so on. But however inadequate or unworthy we may be, in His hand we can all be "tools in the Master's use."

"The foolishness of God is wiser than Men; and the weakness of God is stronger than men."

(*1 Corinthians 1:20*).

Feb 2

May you know the Lord's healing touch

Every one of us can be the recipient of God's healing touch for all of our emotional, physical or spiritual problems. First, however, we must have faith. Faith is the unshakeable certainty deep within our heart. It knows beyond all doubt that each and every one of us is very important to God.

It knows that He truly cares what happens in our lives. When we then, in faith, ask God to heal our pain, He will hear. As our loving Father who wants to give all good things to His children, He will answer. He will heal.

Feb 3

Let There Be Light!

Each day is a resurrection
From the shrouded veil of night...
An affirmative declaration
That God still turns on the light!
Clay Harrison

Feb 4

He Lights Our Way

When we can't see the road ahead
Or know which path to take,
Our God is faithful and sincere
To light our journey's way.
Our steps are lightened by His love
And seasoned by His grace.
Each new day belongs to Him,
To Him belongs the praise.
Without God's touch upon our lives,
Our future would be dim...
But we have faith to see us through;
We've placed our trust in Him.
Jill Lemming

Feb 5

When you think God has thrown a roadblock in your path, whether it comes in from illness or an accident or a lost job, look again. It may be only a jog in the road, a short detour leading to a real fulfillment.

#

If the world seems cold to you, kindle fires to warm it.

Feb 6

It may never be more blessed to give than to receive, but for everything given, there has to be a receiver, And unless the receiver is willing, the blessing to which the giver is entitled is lost.

Feb 7

We can never fall below the reach of God's love.

#

Worry energy can be converted into prayer power.

Feb 8

I Thank Thee

I thank Thee Lord
For my first cup of coffee
For the herbs and spices
That enhance every meal
For the fruits of the garden
The wheat in the fields
For the sun, the moon
The rain and the stars
For the babbling brook
The songs played on guitar
For the lovely seasons
And the sky so blue
But most of all
Because I have You.
Jo March

Feb 9

Back into the Fold

As Christ entrusted His apostles with the task of leading others into the Christian faith, so He entrusts us with the same task today, according to Canon R.C. Stephens

In order that the greatest number of people should hear His message, Jesus enlisted helpers. He made friends with fishermen from the Sea of Galilee, called them to become "fishers of men" (*Mark 17:1*) ; and sent them out in twos to help Him.

Once He sent seventy followers "into every city and place, whither He himself would come" (*Luke 10:1*), and this policy of preparing the way for His visits must have contributed to His popularity and been partly responsible for the crowds which came near Him. Jesus cared not only for their spiritual needs but also for their general welfare – even feeding them when He thought they might faint by the way (*Matthew 15:32*).

I have often wondered what happened to the thousands of people who came to know Jesus – children, those He cured and many others mentioned in the Gospels. At first it certainly seemed that they were likely to be forgotten and left on their own with no one to care for them after Jesus had returned to Heaven. For although He showed Himself to His apostles after His resurrection on several occasions, there remained doubts in their minds, and seven of them actually returned to their former work of fishing, presumably thinking that they would no longer be required as apostles.

Fortunately, Jesus called them back to Himself and told St. Peter to "Feed My lambs; Feed My sheep" (*John 21:1-17*), which surely included people like Martha, Mary, Lazarus, Zacchaeus and many others, showing that those who had come to love Him during His ministry were to be looked after, otherwise they would drift away. St. Peter, as leader, was commissioned to shepherd the flock Christ had gathered during His three years.

Today there must be many who have been brought up in the Christian faith but whose relationship with Christ never developed – perhaps even Sunday school teachers, choiristers, and churchwardens, who later for some reason "fainted and were scattered abroad, as sheep having no shepherd" (*Matthew 9:36*). And there are those who through illness and age who

have been forgotten. It is the task of every Christian to seek
them out and bring them back to the fold.

Feb 10

Father,
Let me hold Thy hand,
And like a child,
Walk with Thee
Down all my days,
Secure in Thy love and strength.
St. Thomas a Kempis

Feb 11

Our Refuge

When times are dark and dreary
And no one seems to care
Our Savior is our refuge,
If we go to Him in prayer.
He's always near to help us
And make our burden light.
It's like a ray of sunshine
Even on darkest night.
Clara B. Plotner

Feb 12

After the Darkness

After the darkness,
The daylight shines through.
After the showers,
The rainbow's in view.
After life's heartaches,
There comes from above,
The peace and comfort,
Of God's healing love.

Feb 13 * *

Best Friend

The Lord is my refuge
My Haven of "Rest"
He shields and protects me
When faced with "Life's Tests."
I go to Him always in prayer for release,
He never forsakes me
But gives me His "Peace."
I fret not – nor worry
Burdens are laid at His feet –
I trust and obey Him
Whenever we meet!
Be happy – not fretful

Be glad and not sad,
The Lord is my "Keeper"
The "Best Friend" I have!
Karen Weisenhoefer

Feb 14

We thank you, God, that in Jesus our sins are forgiven, forgotten, and erased. Help us to accept and believe, so that we may continue to experience your forgiving grace through Christ, our Savior and Lord. Amen.

Feb 15

In the quiet of that hour
When alone with Christ I pray,
I find peace which passeth knowledge,
And His strength for all my day.
For I know He loves to listen
To the things that me distress,
And He patiently gives wisdom,
And His words, my heart do bless.
In the quiet of His presence,
There, my soul in rest does hide
From the evil that doth press me
In this world of sin, so wide.

Feb 16

Trouble –

The structural steel that goes into building character

#

Luck is where preparation meets opportunity.

Feb 17 ***

Our Instinct for Survival

Canon R.C. Stephens looks at the question of life after death
There is one certain fact in this world and that is, we shall all die. And yet our most powerful instinct is self-preservation – we want to live, not die – and we protect ourselves from danger. So strong is this that when we are desperately ill, even unconscious, we continue the fight to survive.

We all have this vital instinct and yet it seems to bring us to a dead-end, something I find hard to accept. I cannot believe that God would have endowed us with such a longing to live if it was bound to end in a cul-de-sac. In a book, *The Wisdom of Solomon*, written in the century before Christ, the author said, "God created man to be immortal, and made him to be an image of His own eternity." God intended our determination to live to extend beyond this world into the next. It is sad that many do not know this and are content to die.

Christ came to earth to do many things – to show us what God is like; to teach us; to take away our sins; to save us; but more than anything He came to give eternal life, not to a chosen few but to all who have an instinct to live. Jesus said, "I am come that they might have life" (*John 10:10*), and "He that believeth on Me hath everlasting life" (*John 6:47*). The word "life" occurs frequently in St. John's Gospel and ever since, Jesus has revived in men and women the desire to continue living and made the tomb a place of life.

In Rome there are many miles of underground passages called the Catacombs, where the early Christians buried their dead. This might be thought of as a place of gloom and darkness but it is evident that these were used for Baptisms and Holy Communion in time of persecution – turning the tombs into temples for the worship of God and bringing life to new members. By believing in Him, people "die to live" instead of "living to die."

"And this is the life eternal, that they might know Thee the only true God, and Jesus Christ, whom thou hast sent" (*John 17:3*).

Feb 18

I'll Walk With Him

I lift my eyes unto the hills
And know that God is there.
I know He watches over me
And hears my every prayer.
I'll walk with Him through meadows green,
By waters cool and still.
My soul He comforts and restores,
My cup with love doth fill.

I walk with Him through valleys dark
And know that He is there.
My steps He guides, I do not fear.
I'm safe within His care.
His hand in mine, I'll journey on
Be skies bright blue or dim.
I'll know a peace and sweet content
If I just walk with Him.
Beverly J. Anderson

Feb 19

The Lord's Prayer

Our Father, who art in Heaven
Hallowed be Thy name.
Thy Kingdom come.
Thy will be done.
On earth as it is in Heaven.
Forgive us our trespasses,
as we forgive those
who trespass against us.
And lead us not into temptation,
But, deliver us from evil.
For Thine is the Kingdom,
And the power, and the glory,
For ever and ever.
Amen.

Feb 20

Courage does not mean living without fear,
but living beyond fear through faith in God.

#

You are what you have learned from the past,
What you experience today,
And what you dream for tomorrow.

Feb 21 **

Take My Hand

Take my hand, oh Lord I pray
And guide me safely through the day,
Help me to always do what's right;
Help me walk in Thy sweet light.
If pain and sorrow come my way,
Help me to be strong, help me to stay
Steadfast and true, whate'er the need;
Help me to live Thy Holy creed.
No matter what the future brings
By unseen fate or angel wings,
Help me to love and ever be
A shining beacon, Lord, for Thee.

Feb 22

My Prayer at Dawn

I pray this day will brightly shine
With little deeds well done,
And thoughtful love for others,
So that the setting sun
And all the lengthening shadows
Will bring a peaceful rest,
Knowing that God guided me
To truly do my best.
Mary H. Wittner

Feb 23

The value of persistent prayer is not that He will hear us,
but that we will finally hear Him.

# # #

He who laughs . . . lasts

Feb 24

A word fitly spoken is like apples of gold in a silver setting.

# # #

The happiest people don't necessarily have the best of
everything.
They just make the best of everything.

Feb 25

God Never Deserts Us

*God does not fuss or interfere with our lives, explains Canon
R.C. Stephens, yet He is always at hand to help and comfort us*

It is most annoying to be given work to do and then have
someone either looking over one's shoulder to see if it is being
carried out correctly or making suggestions how best to do it.
We much prefer being trusted to do the job, using our imagina-
tion and the benefit of our experience, for most of us like to do
things our way.

It is extraordinary, therefore, that when God asks us to work
for Him, it is the other way around. We want Him to fill in the
details and are rather nonplussed when we are left to use our
own initiative. In other words, what we complain about in others is what we hope for from God.

But God never fusses; He wouldn't have given us the work
in the first place if He had thought us incapable of completing
the task. He doesn't treat us as if we are in kindergarten, but
as mature people, and is prepared to allow mistakes to happen
without interfering. He has given us minds and brains and He
expects us to use them in His service, but that doesn't mean
that He leaves us without assistance, for God never deserts us.

Jesus said that if we loved Him, then God in all his fullness
would live in us (*John 14:16, 23*), and St. Paul wrote, "It is God
which worketh in you both to will and to do of His good plea-

sure" (*Philippians 2:13*). Help from His indwelling Presence is for every Christian and in the New Testament is called 'grace', which is the normal and general equipment of a disciple.

We don't have to ask for God's help, for He is already helping us in everything that is right and good and, if we were convinced of this, we would draw on this inexhaustible supply of power and our lives would be more fruitful for Him. St. Paul asked God several times for special help, and was told, "My grace is sufficient for thee (*2 Corinthians 12:9*).

Feb 26

Eternal Flame

Today I lit a candle
On the altar of my heart,
And I prayed the glow within me
Would ignite a magic spark.
A flame to burn forever
So that always I will see,
A world that's filled with beauty
Because He glows in me.
Chris Zambernard

Feb 27

Daily Prayer

Oh, God, touch my heart today
And cleanse me from all sin.

Put your love and joy inside
And keep it safe within
Till someone comes along
And needs my help
To lift their loads today.
Then may I reach inside my heart
And give love and joy away.
Mildred H. Bell

Feb 28

A prayer is nothing till it's heard
Beyond the highest leaf,
But when it's answered, oh my friend,
How strong is our belief!
An act of love may simply be
A smile, a hug, a kiss...
But it's a joy for all to see
When troubles come like this.

Feb 29

It is in loving, not being loved, the heart finds its quest.
It is in giving, not getting, our lives are blessed.

March

Life is eternal. Death is but the shedding of an unwanted garment.

Mar 1

The Time to Pray

When the sun comes peeping o'er the hills
To herald the approach of day,
And the silvery moon fades in the sky,
Just then is the time to pray.
Ere the toils of life come crowding in
And the day speeds on its flight,
The strength one finds when alone with God
Is sufficient for the fight.
So, I'll steal away while the day is young
And bow at the Master's feet.
I'll ask for the grace He'll give me
To face each trial I'll meet.
He'll fill my soul with peace and joy,
A peace that I could not know
Apart from Jesus, the Prince of Peace,
As on through the day I go.
Elnora Wilson

Mar 2 **

In Him You'll Find Peace

When the spirit is heavy,
And burdened with care,
Be not afraid and,
Know that He's there,
Granting you strength,

To bear, with His grace,
The trials and problems,
That each of us face.
His love will sustain you,
Giving release.
To all anxious thoughts,
In Him, you'll find peace.
Colette Fedor

Mar 3

Forever Near

I fold my hands in prayer, dear God,
And humbly turn to Thee,
You are the Master of my fate,
The dearest Friend to me.
I know You are forever near
To guide and strengthen me,
You are the ballast for my sails,
The wind that sets me free.
I fold my hand in prayer, and know
That come what may You share
My sorrows, pain and sweetest joys
Because You always care.
I fold my hands in faith, and feel
Your Holy Presence fill
My heart and soul with wondrous joy,
And always – always – will.
Vi B. Chevalier

Mar 4 **

CONDEMNATION

Until you've walked
A second mile
In someone else's shoes,
Or stood an hour
In the heat
Of hurts you did not choose;
Until your heart
has felt the sting
Of criticizing tongue,
You cannot taste
The salty tears
A wounded soul has wrung.
Unless you've walked
a moon or more
Along a thorny road,
You cannot feel another's need
To know his trying load.
Roxie Lusk Smith

Mar 5

The Spirit of Acceptance

Rev. Dr. David M. Owen urges us to accept people for what they are, and not seek to change them.

When Cardinal Roncalli (*Pope John 23rd*) heard that he was likely to become Pope, he simply placed himself in God's hands, and then felt able to face the tremendous task with an easy mind. He had learned the spirit of acceptance.

Acceptance is a requirement of life, and where it is missing there is likely to be trouble and heartache. I am not suggesting that we should accept in stoical, fatalistic fashion situations that befall us which can be reversed by positive action, but I *am* saying that we can destroy ourselves and damage our relationships by resisting or resenting occurrences and responsibilities which cannot be removed.

So often we are called upon to help someone accept an ordeal which cannot be avoided, or to help ourselves come to terms with some illness, defeat or disappointment. Do we retaliate in anger or wallow in self-pity, or should we rather accept it as something through which we can minister to others – something which can be dedicated to God?

When William Booth, founder of the Salvation Army, discovered that he was losing his eyesight, he replied, "I have done what I can with my eyes and now I will see what I can do for God and the people without my eyes."

There is another kind of acceptance – the acceptance of one another. St. Paul urged Christians in Rome to "Accept one another as Christ accepted us" (*Romans NEB 15:7*). This philosophy lies at the heart of the Christian's code of behavior.

The home is often a place of conflict, between brothers and sisters and parents and growing children. Society, too, is blighted by conflicts of nationality, color and religion.

Even the Church is, sadly, sometimes divided into denominations, and clashes between individuals can ruin the church's fellowship and hinder its witness. I am quite sure that much of this is due to failure to accept other people both for who they are and what they are.

In his ministry, Jesus accepted the skeptical scholar Nathaniel, the fraudulent Zachaeus, the blunderer Peter, and through the centuries has accepted all types in His service, as He does today. He even accepts you and me just as we are. Shouldn't we do the same for others?

Mar 6

The House of Prayer

The "House of Prayer"
Is no farther away
Than the quiet spot
Where you kneel and pray.
For the heart is a temple
when God is there
As you place yourself
In His loving care.
Helen Steiner Rice

Mar 7

Touch Me in Love

Touch my heart in love, dear Lord,
Touch my heart in love.
Cause it to fill and overflow
With blessings from above.
Command the beauty of Thy Son
To shine upon my face,

That all may see the joy that's brought
By Thy transforming grace.
Glenda Fulton Davis

Mar 8 **

A Light at the End of the Tunnel

There's a light at the end of the tunnel,
There's love that's awaiting me there.
All cares and troubles I will leave behind
As I climb the golden stair.
There's a light at the end of the tunnel,
There to meet my Lord face-to-Face,
And I'll be in the home I longed for,
Saved by His heavenly grace.
Helen Parker

Mar 9

Two Thieves – Two Choices

Just outside the walls of ancient Jerusalem three men hung on Roman crosses – two thieves and an innocent king, Jesus of Nazareth. The thieves continually sneered at Jesus, but not once did he rebuke them. The selfless response did not go unnoticed, for one of the criminals soon stopped his scoffing. Realizing Jesus was indeed the Messiah, he looked into the Lord's eyes and said, "Jesus, remember me when you come into your kingdom." Jesus answered him, "I tell you the truth, today you will be with me in paradise" (*Luke 23:43*).

As we prepare for Easter, let us remember the choices of these two thieves. One reminds us that while none of us deserves God's salvation, it is freely offered to all who repent and look to the Savior. The other reminds us that to look away from Christ is to forsake our only hope of eternal life.

Prayer: Lord of life, thank you that you are able and willing to forgive any of us, anytime, anywhere. Amen – *Roger Herndon*

Mar 10

Prayer for Forgiveness

Almighty and eternal God,
Omnipotent above,
We thank you for your blessings
And gifts of greatest love.
We know we are not worthy
Of the love that You possess,
That strengthens us in sorrow
And brings us happiness.
We know that we are guilty
So many times anew,
And truly do not warrant
All that You give and do.
Forgive us for our faults and sins
That we commit each day,
And open wide our eyes to see
The folly of our way.
Harold F. Mohn

Mar 11

My Walk with God

When my busy week has ended
To the country I will trod
Just to feel the closeness of Him
As I take my walk with God.
Hand in hand from hill to valley
Sweet the smell of fresh turned sod
Sweeter still my joy and pleasure
As I take my walk with God.
Every creature pays Him homage
Trees and flowers bow and nod
In the presence of their maker
As I take my walk with God.
Oh, the rapture of this moment
Guided by His staff and rod
Lifted now are all my burdens
As I take my walk with God.
Albert N. Theel

Mar 12

Life is eternal. Death is but the shedding
of an unwanted garment.

Mar 13

Spreading the Word

Through television and radio, we may all become more familiar with the meaning and message of Christianity, says Canon R. C. Stephens

The programs on religious subjects produced on television and on the radio at times not normally given over to religion have been quite remarkable. They have not always been presented by believers, neither have the views expressed always been orthodox, but when I have mentioned this to other people I have found them full of praise, saying how they helped in their understanding of the gospels and that Christ had become more real to them.

So, St. Paul was right when he wrote, "whether in pretense, or in truth, Christ is preached; and I therein do rejoice" (*Philippians 1:18*). These presentations seem to take Him out of a glass case and bring Him into the hurly-burly of modern life where He has always wanted to be.

By being born as we are, Christ plunged from Heaven into the world to share daily life of God's children. His first disciples saw Him as truly human as they were. Though He was morally and spiritually far above them, this did not set Him apart.

He identified Himself with them and the whole of humanity, though He "was innocent of sin, and yet for our sake God made Him one with the sinfulness of men" (2 *Corinthians 5:21*) and He submitted to John the Baptist's "baptism of repentance" (*Mark 1:4*). But His closeness to them was of little comfort when they saw Him die on the cross. Only when he rose from the dead to be with them always did their hopes revive, and they accepted the mystery that He was both human and divine – Son of Man and Son of God.

Today, through the television screen and the radio set, Christ enters our homes. Though the portrayal of Him must be inadequate, perhaps those who are attracted by His humanity and the perfection of His life may come to know Him as the divine Son of God Who alone can rescue us in our troubles, because He even shares in the consequences of our wrong-doing.

Mar 14 *

Home Sweet Home

Home is where the heart is,
We head that way each day
After hustle and bustle of highways
To arrive safely, we softly pray.
At times when home seems tiresome
We feel we must get away,
But, we hang onto that door key,
No matter come what may.
Oh, it's great to go on vacation,
From place to place to roam,
When we grow tired of roaming
The key screams "Home Sweet Home."
We look forward to a Promised Land,
When life's highways we no longer roam,
To hear the Heavenly Father say,
"My child, come in you're home."
Omega Watson Wagner

Mar 15 *

God Cares!

When His eye is on the sparrow
And each budding leaf that grows;
When He sends the dew each morning
And the sunshine to the rose;
You may know beyond all doubting,
In this trial you're passing through,
God cares...and every moment
He is watching over you!
Keith Bennett

Mar 16

Whenever we talk of Christ,
He is there with us.
When Christians are full of Christ
then the whole world will be full of Christ.

Mar 17 *

In His Steps

Dwell not in the valley of despair,
Waste not another day.
Arm yourself with faith and prayer,
And then be on your way.
Yield not unto temptation

Which leads the soul astray,
But focus on the light ahead
And walk the narrow way.
Your Guide shall always lead you
And shield you from harm's way,
But you must follow in His steps
And listen and obey.
His strength shall never fail you
As you stop awhile to pray,
For at the end of the journey,
Heaven's just a step away,
For all who follow in His steps
And listen and obey.
Clay Harrison

Mar 18

God Has Promised

God has kept His promise
To send the rain and sun,
The splendor of the seasons,
The night when day is done.
Everything we treasure
Here on earth below,
Is given without measure
With love, to thrive and grow.

God has also promised
That one day we shall see
His kingdom and the glory,
For all eternity.
Elsie Natalie Brady

Mar 19 **

Give me Courage to face life's trials
And not from troubles run.
Let me keep this thought in mind
"Thy Will", not "Mine", be done.
And if some wish I do not get
Though I have prayed to Thee,
Help me to believe and understand
You know what's best for me.
I've failed you many times, I know
But when tonight I rest,
I hope that I can kneel and say,
"Dear God, I've tried my best."
Helen Smith

Mar 20 *

Ever Near

Lord, lead me, guide me, walk beside me –
Help me find my way,
For at times I tend to wander
Like a sheep that's gone astray.

Walk with me down every mile
On this road we call "life,"
And when I'm feeling overwhelmed,
Please carry me through my strife.
Guide me with your gentle hand,
Make me sensitive to its touch,
For my way isn't always best
And my will's sometimes too much.
Lead me, walk before me,
Make my path open and wide;
Just show me the way and there I'll stay
To serve you by and by.
Gina Mazzullo Laurin

Mar 21

Clearing the Path

As Christians we are pioneers for God, making the way to Him a little easier for others to follow, says Canon R. C. Stephens

The road to God is always difficult, as St Bernard said: "It winds uphill all the way to the end." But there are obstacles which make the journey harder than was intended, and God wants these removed.

It reminds me of my time as a Rector of a country parish which was criss-crossed by footpaths, many of which had become almost impassable, so that ramblers complained they could no longer walk there. Fortunately, a parishioner was anxious that these ancient ways should not be lost, and with a few stalwarts set about clearing them. Most of the footpaths were naturally steep and boggy but unnecessary obstructions were taken away.

Those who did the work were laughingly called 'the pioneers', which seemed an exaggerated name until I found that the definition of a pioneer is "one who, with other soldiers, prepares a road with shovels, etc., for advancing the main army."

God chose St. John the Baptist to make ready the way for the Messiah, and fulfilled the prophecy of Isaiah: "Prepare ye the way for the Lord...and the rough ways shall be made smooth" (*Luke 3:4-5*). The Baptist urged the people to repent, then the obstacles in their lives would be removed and their hearts would open to Christ's message; without such preparation, the mission of Jesus would have been considerably less successful. An atmosphere of expectancy was created and thousands were eager to listen to Christ, Who taught His bearers that the way to the Father was by Him, for He broke the barriers of sin and death.

As disciples, we too are to be pioneers, making the path through life a little smoother for others to walk. And if what we do for them is out of love and compassion, we shall have made it easier for them to find Him Who is "the Way" (*John 14:6*).

Mar 22 ***

Prayer of Saint Francis

Lord, make me an instrument of Your peace.
Where there is hatred, let me sow love.
Where there is injury, pardon;
Where there is doubt, faith;
Where there is despair, hope.

Where there is darkness, light;
And where there is sadness, joy.
O Divine Master,
Grant that I may not so much
Seek to be consoled as to console,
To be understood, as to understand,
To be loved, as to love.
For it is by giving that we receive,
It is in pardoning that we are pardoned,
And it is in dying
That we are born to eternal life.

Mar 23 *

Today

Oh Lord, I thank You for today
Each perilous hour along the way.
The brilliant dawn and noon's warm rays
The sky at sunset, twilight's haze.
I do not take for granted, God
The seagull and the goldenrod
The sparkling glimmers on the sea
Your loving touches, touching me.
Though, I'm at times preoccupied
With pain and problems sorely tried
Somehow with joy my heart sings out
For this beauty You've brought about.
I've had my share of bliss and sorrow.
But know not if I'll have tomorrow
So, for what we've shared in sweet accord

Today, I thank You, loving Lord.
Polly Thornton

Mar 24

Take Time to Pray

A few moments in the morning
Will put a blessing on your day
And you will find Him helping
Your problems on the way.
Don't ever be too busy
To talk to Him awhile
And you will find you're facing
Each problem with a smile.
Don't let the cares of this world
Steal your joy from you
By keeping you too busy
To see what prayer can do.
Some moments in the morning
Before the start of day,
A special time at noon
Before you're on your way.
And at the close of day
Thank Him for everything
That for you He's provided –
A peace to you He'll bring.
Let nothing interfere
With moments spent with God;
You'll find your life goes better
With joy as your reward.

One Day at a Time, Lord

Helen Gleason

Mar 25

Lord, let me take each day
As coming from you.
To give it back to you,
With your Will complete.
And dear Lord,
Let me be kind.
Let me never be discouraged
Or feel sorry for myself.
Because you stand beside me –
Every day.
Father Joseph McCoy, S.M.

Mar 26 **

You taught me to pray –
Ask in faith, and receive,
You taught me to trust –
Not to fear, but believe.
Please help me remember
In all that I do –
My courage my hope,
And my strength
Are in You.

Mar 27 **

Trust Him

There will always be days
When blue skies seem gray.
There will always be times
When you cannot pray.
There will always be moments
When you feel so alone.
There will always be evenings
When no one will phone.
There will always be sadness
When your heart's filled with pain.
There will always be failures
When all seems in vain.
There will always be God
When you feel at a loss.
Trust Him, my friend,
Whatever your cross.
Helen Parker

Mar 28

An Everyday Christian

Canon R.C. Stephens

Some people believe that religion is like a drug that makes us forget present realities and inequalities and that Christianity is too set apart from our everyday lives. It is true that the Gospel does proclaim that this life is not the end but continues into the next, but to say or think that He is not concerned with earthly problems and conditions is to mis-read and mis-interpret the New Testament.

The thousands who followed Jesus wanted to know how to live their own lives and I don't think that they would have bothered to listen to it if He had only held out to them the promise of a distant future, however bright. Christians have sometimes contributed to this misrepresentation by spiritualizing their Master's teaching and so hiding some of the meaning of His words. For instance, the parable of the Prodigal Son teaches loving forgiveness for all who return to Him, but when this story was first told it must have seemed particularly significant to any in His audience who had a son in 'a far country' and it has a similar significance for some parents today.

Christ's message is for this world and the next and He began His work by speaking of the kingdom as present now – "Repent; for the kingdom of Heaven is upon you" (*Matthew 4:17*). He taught us to pray "Thy will be done, On earth" (*Matthew 6:10*) and described the character of those who would know true blessedness now, who would not be required to do certain things but to be a certain kind of people. For this reason, Christ's teaching is universal and can be understood and applied by all in every kind of situation. The fact that Christianity is not controlled by outward circumstances but by the spiritual character of its members has led to much misunderstanding but it is the most materialistic religion of any and, far from being a drug, the Christian faith acts as a stimulus to us to better this world.

Mar 29

"A man's mind plans his way
But the Lord directs His steps."
Proverbs 16:9

###

Heavenly Father, help me to see beyond today.
Give me the strength and courage
to look at my circumstances in the light of eternity. Amen.
"A cheerful heart is a good medicine
but a downcast spirit dries up the bones."
Proverbs 17:22

Mar 30 **

A Daily Prayer

Dear God, I ask forgiveness
For all the wrongs I do.
I know I am not worthy
Of love bestowed by You
You strengthen and sustain me
In time of my despair.
You give me hope and courage
In answer to my prayer.
I know I am not perfect
and cannot hope to be,

But with your great compassion
I know that You love me.
I thank you God with humble heart
For all You give and do.
There is no day that e're goes by
I do not kneel to You.
Harold F. Mohn

Mar 31

Dear God, forgive us when we let other things crowd you out of your position as Lord of our lives. Help us to focus on You and Your will for us today; in Jesus. Amen
Donna H. Eliason

April

Seeking the best in others,
We find the best in ourselves.

Apr 1

And So To Jerusalem

Rev. Dr. Owen follows the events of Holy Week in the world's most famous city

We may describe Jesus' last visit to Jerusalem for that final and momentous week in which He was to demonstrate His one purpose, as getting to the "heart of the matter"; here Jewish history and religious affairs were centered.

The week began at Bethpage on the Eastern slopes of the Mount of Olives. From where Jesus rode on a donkey into the city (*Mark 11:1-11*), which He planned as a demonstration of His Messiah-ship. Pilgrims were expected to enter the city on foot, and if He had come as a military conqueror, He would have ridden a war horse. But as we know He chose a beast of peace.

On this Thursday evening, Jesus had a meal with His disciples at which the bread and wine He gave them symbolized the following day's events when His body would be broken and His blood shed.

The meal over, Jesus went with His disciples to the Garden of Gethsemane, at the foot of the Mount of Olives. There among the olive groves and in agony of prayer, He wrestled with the prospect of torture and crucifixion (*Mark 14:32-42*).

Arrested in the Garden, Jesus was led to the house of Caiaphus, the High Priest for judgement. The church of St. Peter in Gallicantu (the name means "cockcrow") recalls Peter's three-fold denial of Jesus when the cock crowed three times (*Mark 14:66-72*).

On Friday morning, Jesus was handed over to Roman prosecutor Pontius Pilate, and sentenced to death (*Mark 15:1-15*), and in the courtyard was mocked and scourged. Pilate confronted Jesus in the Antonio fortress, the Roman garrison that guarded the Temple. The "Ecce Homo" convent is a reminder of Pilate's presentation of Jesus to the crowd, in the words "Behold the man" (*John 19:6*).

Jesus then carried His cross through the narrow city streets to the crucifixion; the route is remembered as the Via Dolorosa.

Christians are divided over the site of Calvary and the tomb where Jesus was crucified and buried. But what matters is not the actual site, rather the event which climaxed that traumatic week in Jerusalem, and by which today we celebrate the costly love of Jesus.

Apr 2

I believe!

The stone wasn't rolled
away from the tomb
So that Jesus could leave.
He was already gone.
It was rolled away
so that doubters like me
Could look in and cry,
"I believe! I believe!"
Leroy Thomas

Apr 3

Christ Is Risen

Canon R. C. Stephens reflects on the promise contained in the Resurrection, a promise that has endured since the first century

There must be few people who do not know a little about the Resurrection of Jesus, that He showed Himself on a number of occasions and changed His weak, broken-hearted and hopeless friends into men and women whose lives and preaching "turned the world upside down." What reason can we give for such a change?

First, the knowledge that Jesus was miraculously alive restored their courage and confidence. Secondly, although He told them that He was going to leave them, He promised that His presence would always be with them and that assurance gave them the support they desperately needed.

Thirdly, by leaving them to return to His Father in Heaven, He guaranteed that life didn't end at death but continued into the next world with Him. So, the Resurrection has been accepted by millions as the one event in the history of the world which makes sense of life because it gives purpose to the life now and hereafter.

But the documents recording this great event are ancient and some will ask, "Can we really trust them? Isn't it rather naïve to believe that a man could rise from the dead? Isn't it some sort of legend rather that historic truth?"

It is no use denying the fact that this is an audacious, even fantastic claim, yet Christians of all nationalities and ages have found that He has been with them in joy and sorrow, in temptation and sin, in success and failure. They haven't always obeyed or listened to His voice, but they have been certain of His presence.

What then is the meaning of Easter today? To some it will only be a public holiday; to others, just an account of something that is said to have taken place years ago and is largely irrelevant now; but to Christians, it is as true as the day it happened, and they believe that the Risen Jesus comes, as in the first century, to all who love Him.

Apr 4

Every End is a New Beginning

Every end is a new beginning
like the chapters in a book,
By faith we reach out expectantly
turn the page and take a look.
Each volume has a specific size
each complete in our Lord's sight,
He writes His love in many ways,
in sunny days, through darkest night.
He's cast us each as our life's hero,
it's up to us to act the part,
Find the faith to walk rejoicing,
Sing His goodness in our heart.
Of course, we'd sometimes like to linger
in pleasant resting places,
But time goes on and comes the challenge
of tomorrow's untried races.

Since we cannot see and do not know
The next step He has planned,
Boldly make a new beginning
And trust the ending to His hand.
Elaine D. Hardt

Apr 5

Eternal life

One of the things people find difficult to believe in is life after death, says Canon R. C. Stephens

The Transfiguration of Jesus (*Luke 9:28-36*) is celebrated on 6th August and in some places it is considered to be as important as most other major festivals. It was a strange happening and as it was so mysterious, it has been ignored by some and dismissed by others as fiction, but it is part of the Gospel and reveals what otherwise would be hidden. Christ was transfigured while praying on the mountain, and "the fashion of His countenance was altered, and His raiment was white and glistening". The veil separating the earthly and the spiritual was temporarily drawn aside, helping us to answer some of the questions which so often arise in our minds.

In spite of the assurance given by Jesus, each generation asks about life after death – in this incident He spoke with two Old Testament characters, Moses and Elias, who had died centuries before and who were alive in the next world. There can be no greater evidence than this of the reality of the spiritual world and the life to come.

The subject of the conversation of the three was Christ's approaching death at Jerusalem and there was no suggestion that

He could avoid all its pain. And for us, suffering will not necessarily be taken away, nor are we to bear it stoically, but it can be transformed through our belief in Christ to become fruitful and help us. But not everyone finds living worthwhile; a woman, who still has her health and strength, told me that she no longer wanted to live, and a man remarked to me, "What can I do? I'm so bored." It is very sad that some people are weary of living, but life would no longer be dull if we were to meet Christ in our prayers and worship, for He teaches that within everything there is glory which was seen by the apostles on the mount, though it is often hidden from us. For those with eyes to see, "the whole earth is full of His glory" (*Isaiah 6:3*).

Apr 6

A Glorious Gospel

Thought for Today: ...our Savior Christ Jesus, who abolished death and brought life and immortality to light through the gospel." (*2 Timothy 1:10*)

This glorious message of the gospel, written by Paul to Timothy, comes from heartfelt conviction and is a source of uplift and comfort to sorrowing hearts.

Physical life, at best, is uncertain and filled with fears and problems which overwhelm us. This message tells us that we need not let fear of death or destruction darken our lives. Death has been abolished! The gospel proclaims that because He lives, we too shall live (*John 14:19*).

The glorious Good News which we preach is not a pious hope that we shall somehow survive after a fear-ridden journey through "the valley of the shadow." Ours is a proclamation of the truth that "Death is swallowed up in victory." So, we all can join Paul in the joyous shout, "Thanks be to God, who gives us victory through our Lord Jesus Christ!"

Prayer: Dear Lord, we pray that we may have the assurance of the resurrection with us each day of the year. Amen –*Jack E. Jones.*

Apr 7

Christ's Parting Gift

Christ's peace is a certainty in the midst of life's struggles and strife, says Canon R. C. Stephens

A reader who for personal reasons did not give her name and address, has asked me to deal with her problem in a weekly article: she has had some experience of God's peace but it doesn't last long, "Is it perhaps something that grows with time?" she asks.

First, we need to know what is meant by 'peace.' The world considers it to be life without war, trouble and suffering. Those who seldom give a thought to God often complain when the serenity of their lives is disturbed or upset by sickness and disaster and say that there cannot be a God otherwise He would never allow such things to happen.

Jesus made it clear that what He offered was quite different: "Peace is my parting gift to you. My own peace such as the world cannot give" (*John 14:27*). The difference is explained by the Greek word used in the Gospels, which means 'unity brought together' which has nothing to do with freedom from strife and trouble.

The tranquility of Jesus came from His living close to His Father, but the insults, His betrayal and sufferings were not taken away – these He had to endure. Such 'unity' was not easily won, and in Gethsemane we see the intensity of the conflict: "Oh My Father, if it be possible, let the cup pass from Me: nevertheless not as I will but as Thou wilt" (*Matthew 26:39*), and from the garden He went out to face His enemies.

So, Christ's peace is not a comfortable, cozy feeling with everything running smoothly, but a sureness and certainty in the midst of the storms and strife of life. The apostles struggled against giving in to their Master; they complained and criticized, and only after the Pentecost, when they were willing to be governed by His spirit, did they know that "peace which passeth understanding".

As long as we refuse to seek to do God's' will, we shall be at war within ourselves, but as we persevere and invite Him into our lives we begin to be conscious of His peace, which "grows with time" – time we devote to trying to do His will.

Apr 8

> O, dear Lord, three things I pray:
> to see Thee more clearly,
> to love Thee more dearly,
> follow Thee more nearly...
> day by day ...... by day
> ....by day!
> (from *Godspell*)

Apr 9 *

This I Know

I know not what tomorrow brings,
Nor do I fret and fear,
For be it better or for worse,
I know that God is near.
I know if I succeed in life
God will be there to show and lead
And help me start anew.
One thing is certain, this I know,
My faith is strong and true,
And God will always light my way
Each day my whole life through.
Harold F. Mohn

Apr 10

The Sign of Triumph

Ever since Christ was crucified, the cross has acquired a deep significance for Christians throughout the world, says Canon R. C. Stephens

When Christ's enemies demanded a sign, they wanted proof that He was the promised Messiah; this was refused and instead they were told, referring to the prophet Jonah, that the sign would be death followed by resurrection. St. Paul, faced with the same demand, said that he proclaimed "Christ crucified" (*1 Corinthians 1:23*) and within a few years the cross became the symbol of the Christian faith and Christians scratched it on prison walls as they waited for martyrdom.

No word has ever contained a greater depth of meaning, and it puts the Gospel in a nutshell. It shows Christ's sacrificial love in dying for us, and His example has inspired men and women ever since to give their lives for others, as every village and town memorial testifies. "Greater love hath no man than this, that a man lay down his life for his friends" (*John 15:13*). We may not be called upon to die for Christ, but we are required to give ourselves in unselfish service to our fellows.

But the cross is much more than the sign of sacrifice – it also proclaims victory. Christ died but rose again, showing that He had conquered sin and death and that by His power and grace we can do the same. The empty cross is the sign of triumph defeating despair, death and sin; that shameful object, fit only for criminals and ridiculous to those who think themselves wise, brings life and hope. These facts cannot exhaust its message, for the whole Christian faith flows from the cross, as millions have joyfully discovered.

Today the cross is seen everywhere. It beckons us to respond, pointing the way – the only way – to a really satisfying existence. To ignore it is to be deprived spiritually, just as to ignore a 'one way' traffic sign leads to chaos. The cross is the silent witness that love never dies and hope always lives.

Apr 11 *

The Source of Every Blessing

The source of every blessing
Is God, Who reigns above;
A God of love and mercy
And never failing love.
He blesses us with sunshine
And rain to make things grow,
He is there in Autumn's colors
And in Winter's falling snow.
He is there when health is failing
And burdens seem too hard to bear;
He reaches out with arms of love,
With compassion and infinite care.
To all who come unto Him,
He will never turn away,
To all who seek for mercy,
He is just a prayer away.
Francis Culp Wolfe

Apr 12 *

My Unseen Guest

God walks the trail with me each day,
He is my Friend, my Guide,
However long or steep the road,
He's ever by my side.
He sits with me in evening's hush;

We speak, we laugh, we pray,
And my heart sings a joyful song...
He's never far away.
And through each day and dark lonely night,
He's guarding from above.
In perfect peace, I rest secure
In His eternal love.
Lee Simmons

Apr 13

Prayer: Almighty God, we thank you that Jesus conquered death. We rejoice that in Him we can enjoy eternal life. We praise You that when He rose in triumph from the grave, He took the sting away forever. Amen

Apr 14 ***

The Key of Love

Although we live in an affluent world, people still have needs and the greatest of these is to know someone cares. This was brought home to me recently when I had to write to nearly 100 widows, and received almost identical replies saying: "It's wonderful that someone cares." Supplying material needs is not sufficient, however, for there are also spiritual and intellectual worries which must be dealt with if we are to live fully.

People want to be assured that God cares, and this is expressed in three words, "God is love."

(*1 John 1 4:8,16*), found only in St. John's letter. It is sad with so much evil and horror in the world, some people are unable to bring themselves to believe the truth of these words, which state the fundamental principle of the whole universe and without which the world is a sinister place lacking in purpose.

Others are bewildered by the paradoxes and seeming contradictions in the Scriptures. Here again, God's love acts as a lamp, illuminating difficult passages and bringing new meaning and understanding. Love alone can reveal the secrets of God's Word.

Suffering remains a major problem, in spite of all the thought and prayer that has gone into its study, and is a stumbling block to faith, for it appears to be contrary to the spirit of love. Yet only with the key of love is its mystery unlocked to show that He shares our pain, and we can begin to share his sufferings" (*Philippians 3:10*).

If we are honest, we shall admit to being a little afraid of what happens after this life; death is a word we avoid because it seems so final. Love alone can calm our fears and reassure us of "the everlasting arms", and that "through the valley of the shadow of death, I will fear no evil: for thou art with me" (*Psalm 23:4*). It is not enough to believe in a life after this one; we must know that love is there also, and that the words "God is love" are the 'open sesame' to new life.

Apr 15 *

A House That's Built with Love

Without love, a house is just a house –
a ceiling, walls and floor,

But fill that house with faith and love
and it becomes much more.
A home is where your dreams come true
for love abides, you see,
And love makes a house a home
regardless of pedigree.
Home's a shelter from the storms of life
and sanctuary too.
For loved ones wait behind the door
to hug and comfort you.
It's a home where God is honored
And the Bible's often read,
And there the children seek Him
before they go to bed.

Apr 16

A Prayer for Those who Live Alone

I live alone, dear Lord, stay by my side,
In all my needs, please be my guide.
Grant me good health, for that I pray,
To carry on my work each day.
Keep pure my mind, my thought and deeds.
Help me be kind, to meet others' needs.
Save me from harm and malicious tongues,
from pain and fear and evil ones.
When I am sick, in need of care,
O Lord, I pray, that You be near.
When I am low and in despair,
Lift up my heart and hear my prayer.

I live alone, dear Lord, yet have no fear,
Because I know, that You are near.
Amen

Apr 17

Daily Things

Thank you, Lord, for daily things
which mean so much to me –
For the majesty of the morning,
and moonlight on the sea.
Thank you for a job to do,
For a home filled with love –
and thanks for the trials too,
and faith in things above.
Thank you, Lord, for daily prayer,
and friends who come to call –
For the budding rose of springtime,
and the golden leaves of fall.
Thank you, Lord, for April rain
when rainbows fill the sky,
And for the pride inside my heart
when Old Glory passes by.
We praise you, Lord, for eyes that see
when snow begins to fall.
Thank you, Lord, for daily things
Which bless us one and all.
Clay Harrison

Apr 18

Give Us Daily Awareness

On life's busy thoroughfares
We meet with angels unaware –
So, Father, make us kind and wise
So, we may always recognize
The blessings that are ours to take,
The friendships that are ours to make
If we but open up our heart's door wide
To let the sunshine of love inside.

Apr 19 *

This is the Day the Lord has Made

Begin each day with a simple prayer
To let God know you're glad He's there.
Praise Him for the things He's done
As He unveils the morning sun.
Rise and shine; get out of bed,
And thank Him for the day ahead.
Wear a smile don't look depressed
Show the world that you've been blessed.
Stand straight and tall, don't be afraid
For this is the day the Lord has made!
Clay Harrison

Apr 20 *

Open My Eyes

God, open my eyes so I may see
And feel Your presence close to me.
Give me strength for my stumbling feet
As I battle the crowd on life's busy street.
And widen the vision of my unseeing eyes
So, in passing faces I'll recognize
Not just a stranger, unloved and unknown,
But a friend with a heart that is much like my own.
Give me perception to make me aware
That scattered profusely on life's thoroughfare
Are the best Gifts of God that we daily pass by
As we look at the world with an Unseeing eye.

Apr 21

The Courage of Our Convictions

Our response to life should be energetic and enthusiastic, says Canon R. C. Stephens

People often surprise us and ourselves as well. Recently a young woman attended a meeting at which controversial local problems were to be discussed. She had no intention of speaking, but as no one objected to the proposals, she felt compelled to do so and was amazed that so many told her afterwards that they agreed with all that that she had said. So concerned was she that she was brave enough to say so; the others were so half-hearted they didn't have the courage of their convictions, nothing made them say a word. She was like the River Nile, which for most of the year flows normally, but at certain seasons the water near the source builds up and forces it to overflow its banks. The Psalmist said, "I was dumb...my heart was hot within me; while I was musing the fire kindled: then spake I with my tongue" (*Psalm 39:2-3*).

Jesus always admired those who wanted a thing so much that they were driven to vigorous action; there was the widow who was so determined to have justice that she persisted until the judge acted (*Luke 18:2-5*) and the man who wanted loaves for an unexpected guest and knocked up a neighbor to get them (*Luke 11:23*). No one could be neutral – life had to be faced and decisions made – no half-hearted response was acceptable.

Some people put off making decisions, particularly religious ones, and the only way forward is to sit down and think things out to the end. If we do this conscientiously, we shall find power to act because of the spiritual pressure which builds up in our hearts.

The gospel gives a picture of those who are so enthusiastic to get into their kingdom that they jostle each in their anxiety to do so (*Matthew 11:12*). Many show a lack of enthusiasm today due to indecision and half-thought-out life. But a half-hearted response to life is not enough.

Apr 22**

Prayer for Today

Bless all that I may do today,
Oh, may each little task
Be done to minister to those

Who may a favor ask.
I'll pray that I may speak with words
Of Christian charity,
And that my hands be busy with
Appointed work for thee.
The smallest deed, done in Thy Name,
May not man's praises bring,
But they will bless some "little one,"
To honor Christ, the King.
I seek to know Thy guidance, Lord,
That for the hours of my day...
Thy servant, I shall be.
Anna Lee Edwards McAlpin

Apr 23

A Prayer for Patience

God, teach me to be patient –
Teach me to go slow –
Teach me how to wait on You
When my way I do not know ...
Teach me sweet forbearance
When things do not go right
So I remain unruffled
When others grow uptight ...
Teach me how to quiet
My racing, rising heart
So I may hear an answer
You are trying to impart ...
Teach me to LET GO, dear God,

And pray undisturbed until
My heart is filled with inner peace
And I know I am in YOUR WILL!

Apr 24

Oh Come! Let Us Sing!

Oh come let us sing to the
Lord, our Shepherd,
Honor and cheer His holy name!
Come to His presence with
joy and thanksgiving,
Proclaim to all that He does reign!
Our God is great and above all others,
The depths of the earth He does control,
He owns the seas and the
tallest mountains,
For with His hands He's
formed them all!
He is our God, and we are
His people,
So, in His fold forever stay.
Unto His voice we ever
must hearken
Oh, won't you hear His voice today!
Polly Hepting

Apr 25

Angel of God
my guardian dear,
To whom God's love
commits me here,
Ever this day
be at my side,
To light and guard,
to rule and guide. Amen

Apr 26 *

Reach down, oh Lord, and take my hand,
So I may walk where you have planned,
Reach down Oh Lord and dry my tears
That fall like raindrops through the years.
Reach down, oh Lord, and fill my heart
With love that never will depart.
Reach down, oh Lord, and free my soul
Once bound by sin to sorrow's role.
Reach down, oh Lord, and lift my voice
Too long constrained. "Praise Him. Rejoice!"
Marjorie J. Lockhart

Apr 27 **

The Art of Living

There's a special art to living,
And you need a frame of mind
That can overlook the showers,
'Til the sun begins to shine.
To develop to the fullest,
You have got to understand,
That things don't always function
In the way that they were planned.
There's a special art to living,
And the challenge must be met,
But the longer that you try it,
Why the better you will get.
Don't waste your time in waiting
for the world to come to you,
You have to climb the mountain,
To appreciate the view.
Grace E. Easley

Apr 28

A Living Faith

Our religious faith should never be taken for granted, explains Canon R. C. Stephens

No one likes to be taken for granted – yet this is sometimes how we treat our friends. Friendship can only be maintained by communication, by letter, telephone, or visits. Many a friend has been lost through an unanswered letter.

People think that what was theirs years ago will still be theirs today. Couples fall in love and marry and suppose that their love is secure. Later, when a crisis arises and they need to confide in each other, they discover that they have grown apart and are almost strangers. Love is not static, it is living, and as a plant needs nourishment and care, so does love if it is to flourish. Love requires just as much attention after marriage as in courtship.

And what is true of love is certainly true of religion. A man may have a strong belief in God at twenty, but that faith will not be his at fifty-five unless he has done something to strengthen and cultivate it by prayer and Christian experience.

A woman who had been a keen Christian when young and later neglected her faith became seriously ill when she was seventy. As she lay in bed, she struggled to find the faith she thought she still had, but prayer was difficult and God seemed far away – sadly, she realized how far away she had wandered from Him. Frustrated and disappointed, she tried to find her way back. She felt she was like the boy in the parable trying to return home, so she looked in her Bible and came to the words, "But when he was as yet a great way off, his father saw him, and had compassion and ran, fell on his neck, and kissed him" (*Luke 15:20*).

Christian faith can never be taken for granted – it has to be sustained by constant vigilance, otherwise it dies. On the other hand, God cares so much for us that if we have deserted Him and want to return, as soon as we do turn, He rushes to meet us.

Apr 29 *

Carry Me Through

Carry me through today, Lord,
With your gentle wings from above.
Carry me through today, Lord,
Let me feel Your love.
I shall not worry about tomorrow,
Yesterday is gone.
Just carry me through today, Lord,
That's where I belong.
Through all my trials and troubles;
I know that You are there;
Sometimes it's hard to see You
Through each tear and care
Carry me through today, Lord,
Don't let me slip away.
Tomorrow may be taken from me,
So carry me through today.
Margaret Wildflower

Apr 30

Prayer to the Creator

God who raised the vaulted skies
Teach us to be strong and wise.
God who lit the stars above
Ignite in us a steadfast love.
God who guides the wedge of geese

Set us on the path to peace.
God who grew the tall pine tree
Root for us more trust in Thee.
Ruler of the rolling sea
Unveil for us its majesty.
Creator of the world so vast
Lead us gently home at last.
Pauline S. Durgin

May

The best things in life aren't things.

May 1

Walk Beside Me, Hold My Hand

(the voices of special children of God)
Please don't walk in front of me.
It's hard for me to follow things you do.
I need some guidance constantly.
I depend a lot on you.
And if my progress may be slow,
And if I need some extra care,
With faith I'm sure you'll get to know
These are blessings we can share.
And please don't walk in front of me,
Don't push me quickly on my way.
I need your patience, and I plead
That you'll teach me what to say.
I may be known as handicapped.
Some folks say I'm "just not right."
In many ways I don't adapt
But the angels keep me in their sight.
So please accept me this I ask,
Although I'm different from the rest.
The Lord has given me a task:
To show that childlike faith is blest.
Such perfect trust can stir much love.
My innocence is surely planned.
I'm on a mission from above.
Walk beside me, hold my hand.
John and Edna Massimilla

May 2

Oh come, Dear Lord ...

Oh come, dear Lord, I need Thee;
I need Thee so, today –
I need Thy love and guidance
To brighten up my way.
Oh come, dear Lord, I need Thee;
My heart is full of care –
I need Thy strength and courage;
Come, Jesus, hear my prayer.
Oh come, dear Lord, I need Thee;
I need Thee by my side –
Sometimes I feel so lonely;
Come, Savior, and abide.
Oh come, dear Lord, I need Thee;
Let all Thy blessings rain –
I need Thee, Lord and Master,
To wash away my pain.
Oh come, dear Lord, I need Thee;
Fill me with life divine;
Come, take my will and cleanse me,
And make me ever Thine!
Hope C. Oberhelman

May 3

Don't Let Me Falter

Oh Lord, don't let me falter –
Don't let me lose my way;
Don't let me cease to carry
My burden day by day ...
Oh Lord, don't let me stumble –
Don't let me fall and quit ...
Oh Lord, please help me find my "job"
And help me shoulder it.

May 4

A Caring Thought

There is no greater pleasure
Than to help a friend in need,
The simple act of kindness
A smile a word a deed.
A little comfort given
To those who are alone,
A little thought for others
To their needs and not our own.
Dolores Karides

May 5

A Mother's Love

There is no substitute for loving care within the family, explains Canon R. C. Stephens, for a happy home produces happy and well-adjusted children

In spite of cynical comments to the contrary, the making of a happy home is far more important and rewarding than either making money or being successful, and this depends very largely on the way the children are brought up.

Although Christ's ministry was chiefly concerned with adults, it is surprising that the Gospels record so fully His teaching about children, for no other in contemporary literature does so. He had definite views on them and spoke of their significance in the kingdom of God, saying that no one should hinder them coming to Him, for they were the kind of people to whom the kingdom belonged.

He defended their simplicity, and vigorously condemned those who broke their spirit, but declared that those who showed them the smallest kindness would not go unrewarded (*Matthew 10:42*). He loved children and was never too busy to give them His attention. The atmosphere of the home at Nazareth is reflected in His teaching.

There are, of course, many happy homes which make a tremendous contribution to the well-being and stability of the community in which we live, although we hear little of them for they are not 'news'. On the other hand, there are homes where children are welcomed as babies but are less welcome as they grow older; and the attention which is their right is denied them, because it interferes with their parents' freedom.

They must be fitted into an adult pattern of life, thus missing many of the joys of childhood. The television set, marvelous as it is, can never replace the story told or read by mother or father; gifts however expensive or wonderful, can never compensate or be a substitute for love and care.

Affection cannot be bought – a fact which some parents learn only when it is too late, and they are disappointed when their offspring want to opt out of society. Unhappiness in the home is caused not so much by lack of material things as by spiritual poverty: that is, living without love.

Each year Mothering Sunday is more popular; may its observance help us all, parents and children alike, to fill the gaps in our relationships with love. Let 'loving our neighbor' begin at home within the family.

May 6

Motherhood

Blessed is the mother ...
Who can hold on to her children
While letting them go;
Who puts a tranquil home ahead
Of an immaculate house;
Who knows a kind act will be
Remembered longer than an easy word;
Who really believes
that prayer changes things;
Whose faith in the future
Sweetens the present;
Whose Bible never needs dusting;

Whose sense of humor is alive and well.
Thanks, MOM, for everything you do for me!
Happy Mother's Day

May 7

To Mother on Mother's Day

For all the things you've been to me,
My guardian and my guide;
For truths you have so gently taught
And all the tears you've dried;
For faith and understanding
When I faltered on my way.
I owe you more thanks, Mother,
Than words can ever say.
So on this day that's set aside
Especially for you,
I send a wish for happiness
In everything you do.
May each hour bring you pleasure
Every day of every year –
For all the things you've been to me,
I love you Mother dear.

May 8

A Special Prayer for You

Oh, Blessed Father, hear this prayer
And keep all of us in Your care.
Give us patience and inner sight, too,
Just as you often used to do.
When on the shores of Galilee
You touched the blind and they could see
And cured the man who long was lame
When he but called Your Holy Name!
You are so great ...
We are so small ...
And when trouble comes
As it does for us all
There's so little that we can do
Except to place out trust in You!

May 9

Prayer of St. Theresa

Let nothing disturb thee,
Nothing afright thee;
All things are passing
God never changeth;
Patient endurance

Attaineth to all things;
Who God possesseth
In nothing is wanting
Alone God sufficeth.
Translated by *Henry Wadsworth Longfellow*

May 10

Faith

A farmer lives by faith, that's true.
Seeds once sewn are out of view.
By faith he knows the seeds will sprout,
With faith and tool the grain heads out.
The joy of harvest will then arrive,
And with that harvest faith will thrive.
A Christian lives by that faith, too.
God's Word once planted will surely sprout,
With love and prayer belief bursts out.
The joy of harvest resides in God,
As faithful followers, you prepare the sod.
Keep that faith within your heart.
By words and actions that faith impart.
Tell of the peace God's Word gave you,
The same faithful words are for them, too.
The joy of harvest comes from above,
So spread God's Word with faith and love.
John Bammerlin

May 11

Letting Go

Why is it that I always think
That my way is the best?
Why can't I look beyond myself
And on God's shoulders rest?
Why does my stubborn nature
Want to do things its own way?
God tries so hard to teach me,
But I often go astray.
I really want to listen,
But the world's call is so strong ...
It often overshadows Him,
It tempts me to belong.
But if I want His perfect peace,
I must let go of "me"
And trust in Him for guidance ...
Then I'll find victory.
Frances Gregory Pasch

May 12

A Child's Wisdom

We need to be reminded of the lessons children can teach us, says the Rev. David M. Owen

"Children," said, Aldous Huxley, are remarkable for their intelligence and ardour, for their curiosity, their intolerance of shams, the clarity and ruthlessness of their vision."

If we know anything about children we'll know this is true and beneath the irresistible appeal of their simplicity lies a wisdom that sometimes leaves sophisticated adults speechless.

One little boy asked his father the sixty-four thousand dollar question – "Daddy, who made God?" As his father braced himself to face this theological snorter the boy broke in, "Never mind Daddy, perhaps He made Himself!" I remember reaching that conclusion after reading volumes of theological reading!" Another youngster, asked to explain the difference in the role of the Creator and that of the Savior, did so with stunning brevity: "God puts us down and Jesus takes us up."

The great Albert Einstein was reputed to hold a child's intelligence in high regard. One of his neighbors, the mother of a ten-year old, noticed that her daughter often visited Einstein's house. The child explained: I had trouble with my arithmetic homework. People said that at 112 lives a great mathematician, so I asked him to help me, and he explained everything very well." Alarmed at her child's audacity, the mother apologized to him, but Einstein replied, "You don't have to excuse yourself. I have learned more from these conversations with the child than she has learned from me."

We can be particularly thankful to St. Matthew for highlighting the importance that Jesus Himself attached to children. In answer to the disciples' question, "Who is the greatest in the Kingdom of Heaven?" (*Matthew 18:1*), the evangelist tells how Jesus set a child before them with the warning that unless they became like little children they would never enter the kingdom.

May 13

Mother

Children when they are small pull at your apron strings but,
When they are grown up they tug at your heartstrings.

#

Busy Mom's Prayer

I thought I had no time to pray;
This was a busy day.
But on my knees, cleaning up a mess,
I had to laugh, and then to confess.
I finally found the time to pray –
God works in a mysterious way!
Nancy Owen

May 14

Take time to laugh,
It is the music of the soul.

#

Everyone smiles in the same language.

###

Some people make the world more special
Just by being in it.

May 15

Pass It On

If you receive a welcome smile,
Pass it on to keep it in style.
If you receive a word of praise
Pass it on to ensure it stays.
If you receive a pat on the back,
Pass it on to those who lack.
If you receive a hug from a friend,
Pass it on helping others mend.
If you receive a financial lift,
Pass it on, share your gift.
If you receive a message of hope,
Pass it on so others can cope.
If you receive an abundance of love,
Pass it on praising God above.
If you receive an answer to a prayer,
Pass it on, your blessings share.
If you receive God's blessings today,
Pass them on without delay.
William Bredeson

May 16

In Thy Steps

Lord, help me to be a friend to all
Who need a friend today.
May I comfort and encourage

The ones You send my way.
Lord, help me rise above my pain;
To lend a helping hand.
Give me the words I need to say
To show I understand.
Place within my heart a spark
Until it is a flame
And let it shine within the dark
That all may know Your name!
Teach me, Lord, that I may lead
Some weary soul to Thee,
That I might follow in Thy steps
And your disciple be!
Clay Harrison

May 17

Within the House of God

The church is always open
To worship and to pray,
And give you faith and guidance
To face each newborn day.
Within this holy house of God
You'll find strength anew,
And inner peace will find its way
In mind and soul of You.
Amidst its wall of silence

You'll find God always near,
To help you face each problem
And fill your heart with cheer.
Harold F. Mohn

May 18

Lord, Speak to Me

Lord, speak to me, that I may speak
In living echoes of Thy tone;
As thou hast sought, so let me speak
Thy erring children lost and lone,
O teach me, Lord, that I may teach
The precious things Thou dost impart;
And wing my words, that they may reach
The hidden depths of many a heart.
O fill me with Thy fullness, Lord
Until my heart o'erflow
In kindling thought and glowing word,
Thy love to tell, Thy praise to show.
O use me, Lord, use even me,
Just as Thou wilt, and when and where,
Until Thy blessed face I see,
Thy rest, Thy joy, Thy glory share.
Frances Havergal

May 19

Learning to Forgive

It is easy to feel hatred against those who do wrong, says Canon R. C. Stephens, but we should try to follow God's tolerant attitude

Jesus once remarked that He was called "a friend of publicans and sinners" (*Matthew 11:19*) – a description which has been His glory ever since. His enemies intended it as an insult complaining that He mixed with dishonest people whom the scribes and Pharisees would not allow in the synagogue. Jesus went among these people quite naturally and showed by word and deed that God's love was so great that no one, however evil or unrepentant, could possibly be excluded. This was made quite clear when He chose Judas to "be with Him," making him an apostle. He must have known the kind of person Judas was: his inclusion as one of the 'twelve' showed that He wanted him, loved him and appealed to him to remain loyal. Christ failed to hold him and Judas went out from the Last Supper to betray his Master with a kiss, but Christ's love for Him never wavered.

Today we are made very conscious of the evil that goes on in the world – acts of terror and cruelty are reported daily by the media and it is not uncommon to witness the result of such horrors on our television screens. We are rightly shocked and condemn such events, yet we must never write off those who do such things or think of them as beyond redemption even though it is difficult not to feel bitterness against them! I remember a mother whose child had been killed by terrorists, yet in her sorrow she never gave way to hatred and continued to pray for them – a lesson for us all.

God's love has not changed – those who do appalling things and reject His love – are they included in ours? If the church is to continue the Lord's work, it must welcome the whole world and not only those who happened to be religiously or morally-minded.

May 20 *

A Little Time Each Day

Our mountains can be molehills,
If we take time each day
To go to our dear Father, God,
Who hears us as we pray!
It need not be a church pew,
But silence of one's room,
Where we can go to God in prayer,
But no time be too soon!
So rather than our heartaches
Which can be great indeed,
We need to count our blessings all,
'Tis then our prayers succeed!
For God can lift our burdens,
And tho' they feathers be,
if we but give our cares to Him,
Whose eye the sparrow sees!
So, let us seek our Father,
On each and every day
Who hears our petitions one and all,
No matter when we pray!
Sancie Earman King

May 21

I Thank Thee, Lord

I thank Thee, Lord, for all the things
I take for granted every day.
Please help me show my gratitude
in everything I do and say.
The very air I'm breathing now,
The flowers, birds and trees –
the beauty that surrounds us all,
I thank Thee, Lord, for these.
For all the friends and loved ones
I met on life's pathway,
and especially for Thy endless love,
I thank Thee every day!
Doris A. Orth

May 22 *

A Grateful Heart

Give me a grateful heart, Lord,
For each small favor granted.
As years unfold, may I behold
Life still through eyes enchanted.
Let me find beauty in all things,
Nor be too blind to see
The goodness in my fellow man,
That he would find in me.
Grant that my ears remain attuned

To hear the smallest sigh,
And may I lend a gentle touch
To those less sure than I.
Let me remember lessons learned
And profit from the past,
And may I build a bridge of dreams,
That shall forever last.
Let me rejoice in simple things
I need no wealth to buy,
The scent of pine upon the wind,
A burnished copper sky.
Scarlet roses on the fence,
Sunrise through the trees,
Lord, grant that I may not outgrow
Affinity with these.
Give me a grateful heart, Lord,
Let me be satisfied,
When days are less than sunny
And plans lie at low tide.
For life's a sweet adventure,
That leads to who knows where,
And love was made for sharing,
And hearts were made to care.
Grace E. Easley

May 23

The Great Artist

His canvas is the whole wide world,
The brush, His mighty hand.
His palette made up beautifully –
He's the teacher in command.
His clouds are white and billowy
With a hint of pink and gray,
He paints each slender blade of grass
To make a perfect day.
The flowers are carefully tinted
In shades of red and blue.
The water added, so to match
The sky of azure hue.
Surely such a picture
Could only have been planned
And brought before our very eyes
By God's artistic hand!
Susan Walter

May 24

Trust God

There's never a teardrop
that God doesn't see.
He knows when a sparrow
falls from a tree.
There's never a moment

when God doesn't care.
Never a time when He
won't hear my prayer.

A soft answer turneth away wrath.

May 25 *

Follow me

"Take up your cross and follow Me,
Wherever I may lead.
Your back will ache, your feet grow tired,
And yes, your heart will bleed.
But we shall walk together,
And I will share your lot,
For I am always with you,
And will forget you not."
"Take up your cross and follow Me,
and I will fill your days
With joy that only I can give,
In many precious ways.
So, learn to know me better,
For there are miles to go,
And rest your head upon My heart,
For I have loved you so."

May 26

The Unseen Spirit

As we celebrate Whitsuntide, Canon R. C. Stephens considers the influence of the Holy Spirit on our world

Pentecost, the Jewish harvest festival, also commemorated the giving of the Law on fiery Mt. Sinai (*Exodus 20*), so the descent of the Holy Spirit upon the disciples on the day in "cloven tongues like as of fire" (*Acts 2:3*) would be significant. It is difficult to know exactly what took place, but it must have been something tremendous, and extraordinary signs of the Spirit's work are recorded.

Previously, the disciples had relied on Christ's visible presence; now they relied on the unseen spirit in Whose coming Jesus Himself came to them (*John 14:17-18*). The way the little church accepted this new experience was truly remarkable, and its members became more like their Master through this indwelling Spirit.

We look back across the centuries nostalgically to the spontaneity of the first Christians which seem to have disappeared today, but the Holy Spirit is still working in the hearts of men and women. The change might not be spectacular, and it won't capture the headlines, but quietly and gradually there is spiritual growth in human lives.

There are also signs of awakening in areas of life not normally considered religious, such as the growing desire for a fairer distribution of the world's wealth, and a greater readiness for nations to seek peace. All this is part of the Holy Spirit's work, for this is God's world and everything good is due to His influence and inspiration, generally, as well as in people.

May 27

Lord Jesus,
I give You my hands to do Your work.
I give You my feet to go Your way.
I give You my eyes to see as You do.
I give You my tongue to speak Your words.
I give You my mind that You may think in me.
I give You my spirit that You may pray in me.
Above all,
I give You my heart that in me,
You may love Your Father and all people.
I give You my whole self that You may grow in me,
So that is You, Lord Jesus,
Who live and work and pray in me.
Amen

May 28 **

Father God gave His Holy Spirit to
live with man forever.
God's Holy Spirit will guide us so we
make the right choices;
He will guide us into ALL truth!
The Holy Spirit gives us the power to
Overcome every circumstance of life
As He lives in us.
In heaven Jesus Christ is preparing
A place for each one who gives him
His rightful place in our lives.

May 29 *

Footprints

A man at the end of his life was reviewing
The paths he had traveled. Overall the
smooth places and down the slopes of his life,
he noticed two sets of footprints –
as though Someone was walking beside him.
But over the rough spots and up the steep places
there were only one set of prints.
"Why, Jesus," he asked, "did You
walk with me through all the easy parts of my life,
But, when things got rough it appears I walked alone?"
The Master replied, "It's true I walked
beside you along the smooth places.
But over the mountains and rough places
I knew you would really need me.
That's why I carried you."

May 30

Serenity

Serenity comes from knowing God,
Surrender yourself to Him.
Receive the joys He offers you,
Such happiness within.
He'll walk with you and guide you,

Be always at your side.
And when you feel at such a loss,
To Him you can confide.
Helen Parker

May 31

In Harmony with Nature

There are wonders all around us
To see to touch, to hear –
God's handiwork surrounds us
And reminds us He is near ...
So every time you smell a flower,
Or see a starlit sky,
Or hear a cricket chirping,
Or feel a breeze go by,
Or witness all the splendor
A changing season brings,
You've touched the hand of God above –
The Creator of all things!
Alice Joyce Davidson

June

He who sows courtesy reaps friendship, and
He who plants kindness gathers love.

June 1

Let God Be Your Friend

Patience and desire to understand people are the basis for forming lasting friendships says, Canon R. C. Stephens

Our lives are full of relationships and these vary in degree from deep lasting acquaintances – the difference usually being between really knowing someone and just knowing about them. Many of us have been shocked by the discovery that one they thought responsible, turned out to be otherwise: "I'd never have believed it of him (or her)". One of the saddest things is to find that the partner of a lifetime is almost a stranger.

Friendship only develops when we are less interested in facts about others and begin to share their thoughts, ideals and then their love, all of which require patience and a willingness to understand and this can never be hurried. We lose friends or fail to make them because we will not find the time and take the trouble to show them how much we care.

Jesus called the disciples to follow Him. At first, they probably went out of curiosity because His miracles and parables attracted them. However, some of the prayers were probably frightened when His life was threatened (*Luke 4: 29*) and disappointed that He did not make the best use of His opportunities for worldly success. Yet they stayed with Him and didn't allow these facts to drive them away, and because they spent three years with Him their relationship grew into friendship (*John 15:14-15*).

Knowledge of all the incidents of Christ's life will not necessarily keep our faith alive – we must spend time to know Him as a personal friend. On the other hand, some people have difficulties and doubts about some of the important facts of

Christianity, but this need not deprive them of a living trust in Christ. He knows only too well of our problems and welcomes all who sincerely desire His friendship.

June 2

God Beside Us

God is beside us each step
of the way.
If only we lean on His arm
as we pray.
His love is eternal and help
can be wrought
If faith is applied in each
prayer and thought.

June 3

The Handle of the Heart

There is a door to every heart
And yet alas, my friend,
There's but a single handle
And that one is within.
The outside is not fitted
With any lock or key,
And though the Lord
May stand and knock,
The rest is up to you.

June 4 ***

Prayers Can't Be Answered
Unless they are Prayed

Life without purpose
is barren indeed –
There can't be a harvest
unless you plant seed,
There can't be attainment
unless there's a goal,
And man's but a robot
unless there's a soul...
No ships will come in,
if we send no ships out,
And unless there's a contest,
nobody can win...
For games can't be won
unless they are played,
And prayers can't be answered
unless they are prayed...
So whatever is wrong
with your life today,
You'll find a solution
if you kneel down and pray.
Not just for pleasure,
enjoyment and health,
Not just for honors
and prestige and wealth...
But, pray for a purpose
to make life worth living,
And pray for the joy

of unselfish giving,
For great is your gladness
and rich your reward,
When you make your life's purpose
the choice of the Lord.

June 5 ***

On the Wings of Prayer

Just close your eyes
and open your heart
And feel your worries
and cares depart,
Just yield yourself
to the Father above
And let him hold you
secure in His love –
For life on earth
grows more involved
With endless problems
that cannot be solved –
But God only asks us
to do our best,
Then He will "take over"
and finish the rest –
So, when you are tired,
discouraged and blue,
There's always one door
That is open to you –
and that is the door

to "The House of Prayer"
And you will find God waiting
to meet you there,
And "The House of Prayer"
Is no farther away
Than the quiet spot
where you kneel and pray.

June 6

The Handle of the Heart

Never be discouraged
When failures come to light –
Just use them for stepping stones
And make a stronger fight.
Loreta Inman

June 7

MONEY –

What we hang onto,
we are responsible for.
What we give to God,
He's responsible for.

June 8

The Holy Spirit

Canon R. C. Stephens reminds us that the Holy Spirit is always close at hand ready to help us

When St. Luke wrote the Acts of the Apostles, he used two significant words to describe the coming of the Holy Spirit at Pentecost – wind and fire. "There came a sound from heaven as of a rushing and mighty wind, that filled all the house where they were sitting. And there appeared unto them cloven tongues like of fire" (*Acts 2:2-3*). It may be difficult for us to imagine what actually took place, but there is no difficulty in understanding the results of His coming, for it made God intensely real to the disciples and they were fired with enthusiasm to do His will. Without the visible presence of Jesus, they might have been hesitant and undecided what to do; instead there was certainty and purpose in all their actions. That was a long time ago and Christianity may seem to have lost its fire, yet throughout the world there are Christians full of love for God and for other people.

Theodore Parker, a great American preacher (*1810-1860*), once told how as a child he began to know God. Going home from school, he passed a lake where a turtle was basking in the sun. Immediately he picked up a stone to throw at it but a voice within him said, "Don't do it." He was so startled that he dropped the stone and ran to ask his mother, "Who was it?"

She replied, "It must have been the Holy Spirit, and Theodore cried, "Is God as real as that?" We may never have an experience like Pentecost for God does not always come "like as of wind and fire", he also comes in the "still small voice" (*1 Kings 19:12*).

Jesus spoke of His apostles as the Advocate. "Your Advocate, who will be with you forever – the spirit of truth" (*John 14:16*). 'Advocate' is the translation of a word which meant 'one called alongside'. So often the Holy Spirit is thought of as vague and shadowy but we must remember that always He is there by our side, waiting for us to ask for His help.

June 9

Give us Lord a pure heart that we may see Thee,
A humble heart that we may hear Thee,
A heart of love that we may serve Thee,
A heart of faith that we may live Thee.
Dag Hammerskjold

June 10 **

The Winding Road

There is a road that leads uphill,
Past streams and flowers fair,
Above the valley of yesterday
And past the bridge of care.
It's a long and winding road,
Where sun and shadows blend,
Where never a footstep falters
And every grief must end.
There is a road that leads uphill,
A million miles from pain,
Where heartache is a stranger

One never meets again.
Where golden dawn replaces night
To mark the journey's end,
Where Jesus waits beside the gate
...To bid us enter in.
Grace E. Easley

June 11

Pack Away Your troubles

Face your day with a happy heart
And end it with a song –
You'll find the hours in between
Can't go far from wrong.
A smile is more contagious
Than a dreary frown,
And nicer to remember
When the sun goes down.
Don't miss out on happiness
By looking at the ground –
But keep looking skyward,
That's where the rainbow's found.
Just pack away your troubles
For another day
And before you know it,
They'll have slipped away.
Catherine Janssen Irwin

June 12

This is All I Ask

Lord, show me the way
I can somehow repay
The blessings
You've given to me...
Lord, teach me to do
What You most want me to
And to be what You
Want me to be...
I'm unworthy I know
But I do love You so –
I beg You to answer my plea...
I've not much to give
But as long as I live
May I give it completely to Thee!
Helen Steiner Rice

June 13

The World Needs Friendly Folks Like You

In this troubled world
it's refreshing to find
Someone who still has
the time to be kind,
Someone who still has
the faith to believe
That the more you give

the more you receive
Someone who's ready
by thought, word or deed
To reach out a hand
In the hour of need.

June 14

The Coming of the Spirit

The Apostles placed their trust in the Holy Spirit and we should do likewise, says Canon R. C. Stevens

The disciples must have had a wonderful time sharing Christ's life – miracles one day – discussions with scribes the next. Hearing fascinating stories, sleeping under the stars, traveling from place to place, never knowing what a day would bring; everything was unexpected. Jesus did, however, warn them of the of the Spirit's coming so that they were able to take the Pentecost (Whitsun) in their stride. This amazing happening didn't shatter their composure: immediately afterwards St. Peter with business-like efficiency preached to the people and 3,000 were added to the group of believers (*Acts 2*).

The Apostles had, of course, to adjust to new conditions – Jesus was no longer there to tell them what to do. They were on their own – although not really, because the Spirit was with them. They gave Him full rein over their lives and the affairs of the Christian community. This brought difficulties of the unforeseen – without warning He sometimes took over while they hesitated (*Acts 10:44*) and He stopped St. Paul preaching in Asia (*Acts 16:6*).

Sir Anthony Conan Doyle once wrote a story telling how supply of air suddenly ceased and consequently every living creature collapsed. The Holy Spirit sustains us and we know that God would never take Him from us, but we often act as if He had. Like Nicodemus perhaps we are worried by the uncertainty of "the wind" that "bloweth where it listeth...so is everyone that is born of the Spirit" (*John 3:8*).

With such lack of faith can it be wondered that many Christians fail to show that abundant life which Jesus promised? We must therefore renew our belief in the Spirit's Presence and so prepare ourselves for His demands.

Christians are showing greater interest in the Holy Spirit than they have done for many years – so perhaps revival is on the way.

June 15

Request

To turn this troubled
longing into prayer
To smile and place the
future in His care;
To think of others, cheer their
burdened hearts –
To let no sin divide from
Thee apart;
To sing when nature urges to
complain, –
To help some soul, through Christ
to health again,

To work, when pleasure calls,
alluring ever,
And to be kind and true
dear Lord, – forever.

June 16

God!

The power that heals,
The love that protects,
The wisdom that guides,
The freedom that finds,
The yearning that fills
The inspiration that creates,
The action that produces,
The concern that restores...
The Spirit knows the journey
And ever lights the way.
Roxie Lusk Smith

June 17

A blessing for Sitting (*Acts 2:1-4*)

Thought for Today: "Dead wood can make a great blaze if it comes into contact with a flame." *David Mains*

When the Holy Spirit came on the day of Pentecost, the posture of the disciples was particularly revealing. In the upper room, they were sitting. There are some religions in which postures are important in order to obtain a state of religiosity. In Christianity, however, we are not bound by any particular posture in order to obtain communion with God.

Pentecost tells us that we are free to experience communion with God in any place or situation we find ourselves. Whether reading on a bus, vacuuming a house, or meditating in solitude in your prayer closet, God is near. Pentecost loosed our faith from any legalistic system of obtaining communion with God. The result is, of course, a realization that closeness to God can be experienced anywhere.

Prayer: Heavenly Father, thank you for releasing us to experience you in all of life anywhere we are. In Jesus' name. Amen *Lawrence D. Clark*

June 18 ***

You Helped Us Before,
God, Help us again

"O God, our help in ages past,
Our hope in years to be" –
Look down upon this 'Present'
And see our need of Thee...
For in the age of unrest,
With danger all around,
We need Thy hand to lead us
To higher, safer ground...
We need Thy help and counsel
To make us more aware
That our safety and security
Lie solely in Thy care...

Give us strength and courage
To be honorable and true
Practicing 'Your Precepts'
In everything we do,
And keep us gently humble
In the 'Greatness' of 'Thy love'
So someday we are fit to dwell
With Thee in 'Peace Above".

June 19

With patience as gentle
As that from a dove,
He forgives and restores me
With mercy and love.
Through all of life's pathways
No harm will I fear,
For I know my Shepherd,
He ever walks near.
Kay Hoffman

June 20

With Faith in God

When grief and pain engulf you
And tear your heart in two,
You'll find that God is standing by
To always comfort you.
When clouds of gloom obscure your view

Do not feel great despair,
You'll find an inner strength to cope.
If you seek God in prayer.
As sure as daytime follows night
And sunshine follows rain,
The faith in God that you possess
Is never placed in vain.
Harold F. Mohn

June 21

Tribute to Father

My father was a hero
Who never won a medal.
Awards are not given for men who
Get up and go to work
Day after day after day
At hard and tedious jobs
To provide for their families;
Who wake up in the middle of the night
To comfort a child who is sick
Or frightened by a nightmare;
For men who take their children fishing,
To ball games and piano lessons
And go with them to church.
My father was a wealthy man
Who never had much money,
But he had a heart of gold
And a million-dollar smile,
which he shared generously

along with a few dollars
he had in his pockets.
He also had a rich supply of stories
That delighted his children.
This brave, strong, gentle wonderful man
Never got his fifteen minutes of earthly fame,
But I'm confident his name is known in heaven.
Mary Blair Immel

#

Happy Father's Day!

"The most important thing a father can do
for his children is to love their mother."

June 22

Fill Your Heart with Thanksgiving

Take nothing for granted,
for whenever you do
The "joy of enjoying"
is lessened for you –
For we rob our own lives
much more than we know
When we fail to respond
or in any way show
Our thanks for the blessings
that daily are ours...
The warmth of the sun,

the fragrance of flowers,
The beauty of twilight;
the freshness of dawn,
The coolness of dew
on a green velvet lawn,
The kind little deeds
so thoughtfully done,
The favors of friends
and the love that someone
Unselfishly gives us
in a myriad of ways,
Expecting no payment
And no words of praise –
Oh great is our loss
when we no longer find
A thankful response
to things of this kind,
For the joy of enjoying
and the fullness of living
Are found in the heart
that is filled with thanksgiving.

June 23 * * *

Bless me, heavenly Father,
Forgive my erring ways
Grant me strength to serve Thee,
Put purpose in my days...
Give me understanding
Enough to make me kind
So I may judge all people

With my heart and not my mind...
And teach me to be patient
In everything I do,
Content to trust Your wisdom
And to follow after You...
And help me when I falter
And hear me when I pray
And receive me in Thy kingdom
To dwell with Thee some day.

June 24

The Lord is My Shepherd

The Lord is my Shepherd,
And I am his lamb,
Who loves me in spite
Of the way that I am.
Who sees something in me,
That other folks miss,
And sometimes think maybe,
Because of this
I've never felt bitter,
Unloved or alone.

June 25

Always remember to forget
The troubles that passed away.
But never forget to remember
The blessings that come each day.

###

Politeness is a small price to pay
for the good will and affection of others.

June 26

Missed Opportunities

Canon R. C. Stephens urges us to make use of chances to help others

In the stories of the New Testament we can see, unfortunately, many examples of lost opportunities – the inn-keeper at Bethlehem who let go of his chance of welcoming the Savior of the world. Did he realize later what he had done, and would he have made excuses – that he did not know, or that no one had told him? Would Pilate have left a different name behind him had he acted otherwise? (*Luke 23:24*).

Looking back over our life, we can regretfully see many missed opportunities when we could have been of help to friends or neighbors, but we are often unaware of their difficulties, or too deaf to hear them.

Sometimes opportunities are denied us through no fault of our own; when sickness comes and we can no longer give our customary help to others, or when trouble descends and we do not have the means to support those in need. When this happens we feel so useless; yet no one could have experienced such frustration as St. Paul did when he was hindered from doing God's work by suffering and danger (*2 Corinthians 11:23-27*), until he found that God could overrule these, and he found that every trouble brought its chance of serving God.

When opportunities come our way, all we need is to be ready to take them. "As we have therefore opportunity, let us do good unto all men." (*Galations 6:10*).

June 27 ***

Heart Gifts

It is not the things that can be bought
that are life's richest treasure,
It's just the little "heart gifts"
that money cannot measure.
A cheerful smile, a friendly word,
a sympathetic nod
Are priceless little treasures
from the storehouse of God.

June 28

Prayer for Faith

Before I ask, kind Father
Thou knowest of my need;
My courage falleth in the dark,
Stretch forth Thy hand to lead
My stumbling feet o'er rugged paths;
I cannot find the way
Without the help Thou hast to give
My spirit day by day.
Almighty God, grant me to see
The working of Thy will;
May I resign myself to Thee
Retain my peace until
I trust the way Thine hand hast moved
In these affairs of mine.
Renew my faith, that I may see
Thy purposes divine.
Anna Lee Edwards McAlpin

June 29

The Bible says...

"For God so loved the world,
the he gave
His only begotten Son
that whosoever
believeth in Him

should not perish
but have everlasting life."
John 3:16

June 30 ***

Holy Guidance

Let me walk with you, Lord Jesus,
Over all of life's beaten trails;
Guide me through life's shades and shadows
Over paths of least travail;
Lead me by life's great temptations
To your Kingdom, up above;
Lead the way for me to follow,
To Your world of peace and love.

July

*When you become reluctant to change,
remind yourself of the beauty of Autumn.*

July 1

An Historical Prayer for Our Land

Almighty God,
Who has given this good land for our heritage,
we humbly beseech Thee
that we may always prove ourselves
a people mindful of Thy favor
and glad to do Thy will.
Bless our land with honorable industry,
sound learning, and pure manners.
Save us from violence, discord and confusion;
From pride and arrogance
and from every evil way.
Defend our liberties,
and fashion into one united people
the multitude brought hither
out of many kindreds and tongues.
Endow with the spirit of wisdom
those whom in Thy name
we entrust the authority of government,
that there may be justice and peace at home,
and through that obedience to Thy law,
we may show forth Thy praise
among the nations of the earth.
In time of prosperity,
Fill our hearts with thankfulness,
And, in the day of trouble,

Suffer not our trust in Thee to fail;
All of which we ask through
Jesus Christ our Lord,
Amen.

July 2

The New Colossus

... Here at our sea-washed,
sunset gates shall stand
A mighty woman with a
torch, whose flame
Is the imprisoned lightning,
and her name, Mother of Exiles.
From her beacon-hand
Glows world-wide welcome;
her mild eyes command
The air-bridged harbor that
twin cities frame.
"Keep, ancient lands,
your storied pomp!"
cries she with silent lips.
"Give me your tired, your poor,
Your huddled masses
Yearning to breathe free,
The wretched refuse of
your teeming shore.

Send these, the homeless,
tempest-tossed to me.
I lift my lamp
beside the golden door!"
Emma Lazarus

July 3

America's Gospel

Our country hath a gospel of her own
To preach and practice before all the world—
The freedom and divinity of man,
The glorious claims of human brotherhood,
And the soul's fealty to none but God.
James Russel Lowell

July 4

The Nation's Strength

I know three things that must always be
to keep a nation strong and free.
One is hearthstone bright and dear,
With busy, happy loved ones near.
One is a ready heart and hand
To love, to serve, and keep the land.
One is a worn and beaten way
To where the people go to pray,
So long as these are kept alive

Nation and people will survive.
God, keep them always, everywhere,
The hearth, the flag, the place of prayer.

#

An excellent plumber is infinitely more
Admirable than an incompetent philosopher.
A society which scorns excellence in plumbing
because plumbing is a humble activity
and tolerates shoddiness in philosophy because it is
an exalted activity, will neither have
good plumbing nor good philosophy.
Neither its pipes nor its
theories will hold water.
John Gardner
(Secretary of Health, Education and Welfare)

July 5

Hymn

Father, send on Earth again
Peace and goodwill to men;
Yet, while the weary track of life
Leads thy people through storm and strife,
Help us to walk therein.
Guide us through the perilous path;
Teach us love that tempers wrath;
Let the fountain of mercy flow
Alike for helpless friend and foe,

Children all of Thine.
God of grace, hear our call;
Bless our gifts, Giver of all;
The wounded heal, the captive restore.
And make us a nation evermore
Faithful to freedom and thee.
Oliver Wendell Holmes

July 6

Father, we Thank Thee

Father, we thank Thee:
For peace within our favored land,
For plenty from Thy bounteous hand,
For means to give to those in need,
For grace to help in thought and deed,
For faith to walk, our hands in Thine,
For truth to know Thy law divine,
For strength to work with voice and pen,
For love to serve our fellow men,
For light the goal ahead to see,
For life to use alone for Thee,
Father, we thank Thee.
Grenville Kleiser

July 7

Lady Liberty Dedicated

As early as 1865, August Bartoldi considered creating *Lady Liberty*. He and other Frenchmen thought the work could serve as an honor to America and a promise to France.

Bartoldi visited America to see for himself whether freedom was a reality here. He toured the nation admiring democracy at work but found no benefactors willing to finance his dream. Eventually French people gave $450,000.

Bartoldi completed Liberty's arm and torch in time for America's centennial where it became a major attraction.

But, as the statue neared completion in France, funds for its pedestal ran out. In America, Hungarian immigrant Joseph Pulitzer ran editorials in the *World* calling for help. Poor and middle class Americans answered with $1 and $2 donations. In all, they gave $350,000 for the pedestal.

New York artists were among those who helped. Manuscripts by Brett Harte, Mark Twain and other writers were auctioned. Poet, Emma Lazarus wrote a poem titled *The New Collossus*.

In the sonnet's final lines Liberty says – "I lift my lamp beside the golden door."

A cannon fired and Bartoldi released the cord. Liberty was at last unveiled.

July 8 *

God is Never Beyond Our reach

God is never beyond our reach.
He's only a prayer away.
Trust Him always, look to His love.
He's watching and waiting today.
When trouble comes and things go wrong
And you've reached the end of your rope,
Just tie a knot and hang on tight.
Look to God, where there's hope.
When skies above seem dark and gray
And clouds promise rain,
Count your blessings, trust in the Lord.
Soon the sun will shine forth again.
When day is done and shadows fall
And the night seems dark and long,
Worry not then O, child of God.
Sleep, for soon cometh the dawn.
His love endures forevermore.
There never was such a friend.
Thus, He stands so eager to help
With courage right to the end.
No God's never beyond our reach.
He's only a prayer away.
Trust Him always, look to His love.
He's watching and waiting today.
Mary E. Harrington

July 9

Give Us understanding

O, God, our help in ages past,
Our hope in years to be,
Look down upon us all tonight
And make us more like Thee.
Gives us understanding,
Enough to make us kind,
So we may judge all people
With our heart and not our mind.
Helen Steiner Rice

July 10

He Cares for Me

Dear Lord, I know you care for me.
How many times I see.
The signs You leave through the day,
To let me know You passed this way.
How could I ever disbelieve,
Who feel Your hand upon my sleeve?
Nor lose my way throughout the land,
Who find Your footprints in the sand?

July 11

"Dear Friends"

We all need words to live by,
To inspire and guide us,
Words to give us courage
When the trials of life betide us –
And the words that never fail us
Are the words of God above,
Words of comfort and courage
Filled with wisdom and with love –
They are ageless and enduring
They have lived through generations,
There's no question left unanswered.
In our Father's revelations –
And in this ever-changing world
God's words remain unchanged,
For through countless ages
They've been often rearranged,
The *truth* shines through all changes
Just as bright today as when
Our Father made the *Universe*
And breathed His life in men –
And the words of inspiration
That I write for you today
Are just the old enduring truths
Said in a rhythmic way –
And if my "borrowed words of truth"
In some way touch your heart,
Then I am deeply thankful
To have had a little part.

In sharing these *God-given lines*,
And I hope you'll share them, too,
With family, friends and loved ones
And all those dear to you.

July 12 * *

Another Day

Lord, thank you for another day,
Within this life of mine.
Give me the strength to live it well,
Whatever I may find.
Bestow from Your abundance,
Whatever I may lack
To use the hours wisely,
For I cannot get them back.
Lord, thank You for another day,
in which to make amends
for little slights or petty words,
inflicted on my friends.
For sometimes losing patience,
With problems that I find,
For seeing faults in other lives.
But not the ones in mine.
Lord, thank you for another chance,
In which to try to be
A little more deserving

Of the gifts you've given me.
For yesterday is over,
And tomorrow's far away,
And I remain committed,
To the good I do today!
Grace E. Easley

July 13

The Bible Says

"The Helper, the Holy Spirit whom the
Father will send in my name,
Will teach you everything and make you
remember all I have told you."
John 14:26

July 14

What is Love?
It's silence when your words would hurt,
It's patience when your neighbor's curt.
It's deafness when the scandal flows,
It's thoughtfulness for another's woes.
It's promptness when stern duty calls,
It's courage when misfortune falls.

July 15 ***

It's me again, God

Remember me, God?
I come every day
Just to talk with You, Lord,
And to learn to pray ...
You make me feel welcome,
You reach out Your hand,
I need never explain
For You understand ...
I come to You frightened
And burdened with care
So lonely and lost
And so filled with despair,
And suddenly, Lord,
I'm no longer afraid,
My burden is lighter
And the dark shadows fade ...
Oh, God what a comfort
To know that you care
And to know when I seek You
You will always be there!

July 16

God's Garden

As a garden has to be tilled before it will produce crops, so we have to be prepared before we are ready to follow Christ, says Canon R. C. Stephens

The main purpose of a garden is to produce crops but no gardener makes the mistake of thinking that seeds or plants will grow unless the ground is tilled. Similarly, the early Christians had to spend time telling the people all about Jesus before they could expect them to become followers as well. When we read "you are God's garden" (*1 Corinthians 3:9*), St. Paul and Apollos had already prepared the Corinthians to receive the gospel.

In the Parable of the Sower (*Luke 8:4-15*) four kinds of soil are mentioned but only one brought forth a harvest. What the story does not say is that the poor soils can be improved and that the good ground can revert to unproductiveness. Likewise, shallow lives can be deepened by prayer and service as the soil on the rocky island of Aran was deepened by the inhabitants scraping earth from between the rocks. And we all know how to deal with weeds – we have to keep in check the spiritually useless things in our lives.

Probably the hardest lesson we have to learn is the need for constant attention if the ground is to remain in 'good heart'. We must keep the 'fork' of praying going all the time to let in God's light and the 'hoe' of discipline moving to control the weeds – and then the seed will bring forth harvest.

July 17

Food for Thought

Two buckets passed each other in a well
The first one grumbled,
"no matter how full I go up,
I always come down empty."
The other replied,
"No matter how empty I go down,
I always come up full."

###

Worry does not empty tomorrow of its sorrow;
it empties today of its strength.
Corrie Boon

July 18

O God, who art even beyond
the uttermost reaches of space,
help us to recognize Thee everywhere.
Father, who has made us in Thy image,
encourage us to approach Thee
In Spirit and Truth.

July 19 * *

Good Morning, God!

You are ushering in another day
Untouched and freshly new
So here I come to ask You, God,
If you'll renew me, too.
Forgive the many errors
That I made yesterday
And let me try again, dear God,
To walk closer in Thy way ...
But, Father I am well aware
I can't make it on my own
So take my hand and hold it tight
For I can't walk alone!

July 20

Blessing All Our Days

Many blessings be ours in the morning,
May gladness be ours in the night,
May the breezes but gently caress us
And the sun give us softly its light.
In stress and in doubt and in danger
True courage and faith may we know,
And the Home Lights of God be out beacon,
Wherever we stay or we go.
Brian O'Higgins

July 21 **

This is My Prayer

Bless me, heavenly Father,
forgive my erring ways,
Grant me strength to serve Thee,
put purpose in my days ...
Give me understanding
enough to make me kind
So I may judge all people
With my heart and not my mind ...
And teach me to be patient
In everything I do,
Content to trust Your Wisdom
And to follow after you ...
And help me when I falter
And hear me when I pray
And receive me in Thy kingdom
To dwell with Thee someday.
Helen Steiner Rice

July 22 **

Thank You God,
For your promise
That you will never leave us.
Guide us through this life until
we arrive at that Mansion above.

July 23 **

Open My Eyes

God, open my eyes so I may see
And feel Your presence close to me ...
Give me strength for my stumbling feet
As I battle the crowd on life's busy street,
And widen the vision of my unseeing eyes
So in passing faces I'll recognize
Not just a stranger, unloved and unknown,
But, a friend with a heart
That is much like my own ...
Give me the perception to make me aware
That scattered profusely on life's thoroughfare
Are the best Gifts of God
That we daily pass by
As we look at the world
With an unseeing eye.
Helen Steiner Rice

July 24

Let Us Take Time

Let us take time every morning
To turn to our God and say
Thanks for another restful night
And the dawn of a brand-new day.
Thank you for the blessings and gifts
You've given us all these years,

And for the times you've helped us through
Life's many heartaches and tears.
Thank you for this beautiful world –
For the flowers, the birds, and the trees,
And for so many precious children.
We thank you for all of these.
Your blessings and gifts outnumber, by far,
The stars that shine above,
But the one we treasure most of all
Is Your overwhelming love!
Doris A. Orth

July 25

God hath not promised
skies always blue,
Flower strewn pathways
all our lives through;
God hath not promised
sun without rain,
Joy without sorrow,
peace without pain,
But God hath promised
strength for the day,
Rest for the labor,
light for the way,
Grace for the trials,
help from above,
Unfailing sympathy,
undying love...

July 26 *

The Meaning of True Love

It is sharing and caring,
Giving and forgiving,
Loving and being loved,
Walking hand in hand,
Talking heart to heart,
Seeing through each other's eyes,
Laughing together,
Weeping together,
Praying together,
and always trusting
And believing
And thanking God
For each other ...
For love that is shared
Is a beautiful thing –
It enriches the soul
And makes the heart sing!
Helen Steiner Rice

July 27

They say it always seems darkest
In the hours before the dawn,
But joy cometh in the morning
Giving us faith to go on.
Thus, we should trust Jesus always.
Give him each sorrow and pain.

For joy cometh in the morning
Like sunshine after the rain.
Mary E. Harrington

July 28

Daily Prayers Dissolve Your Cares

I meet God in the morning
And go with Him through the day,
Then in the stillness of the night
Before sleep comes I pray
That God will just "take over"
All the problems I couldn't solve,
And in the peacefulness of sleep
My cares will all dissolve.

July 29

Joy in Christ's Teaching

Canon R. C. Stephens says...

We often expect little children to be lively and suspect there is something wrong with them if they are stolid and serious all the time. In the teaching of Christ, there is this same quality of liveliness which is part of its special appeal and importance.

Christ made religion attractive, not only by stressing the need to be joyful and thankful for God's blessings, but also by the manner in which He presented it as the motive-power of our true development. The way to enjoy life and to preserve one's mentality and vigor is to be always looking forward.

You must have met elderly people who refuse to make plans or even hope that they have pleasures and powers still ahead of them. In fact, anticipation and preparation for life's next adventure can be a big contribution to our continuing happiness. There is nothing that will so much accelerate a downhill movement in life as a conviction that everything worthwhile is now behind us and life holds no further joyful surprises or challenges.

Jesus never thought of human life as static, but rather always regarded religion as something dynamic. He sought to recreate human personality by opening a window on the splendor which awaits the children of God. He gave people a vision of the joy that is waiting round the next corner and beyond every twist and turn of the road ahead.

So many of Jesus's parables are concerned with the principle of growth. All is movement and development. Ahead of us, if we are concerned with doing the will of God, is fulfillment. "Beloved, now are we the sons of God, and it doth not yet appear what we shall be" (*1 John: 3:2*).

Just as John the Baptist prepared a way in the wilderness for Christ, so Christ prepares our way into the future and eternity. We "press towards the mark", taking with us into the next stage what is good that has never been given us, certain that one day we shall see their full reality.

July 30

The Grace of God

He gives me hope and courage
To face each newborn day.
He guides me through the shadows
To light and show the way.
He comforts and sustains me
In times of distress.
He gives me inspiration
To find true happiness.
He grants to me forgiveness
When I may go astray.
He helps me in my trials
And does my fears allay.
He never does forsake me
In moments of despair.
And when I need a helping hand,
I always find Him there.

Harold F. Mohn

July 31 *

God's Love

God's love is ever boundless.
It spans a world-wide chart;
Yet reaches down to you and me
And dwells within our heart.
God's love is ever faithful,

Steadfast through every day.
A love that never will forsake –
He'll be with us always.
God's love is never-changing.
He's every day the same.
He loves us now. He always will.
Oh glory, to His Name!
God's love is never-ending,
Lasts through eternity.
Forever and forevermore
His love for us shall be!

Beverly J Anderson

August

Forgiveness is the fragrance a violet sheds
on the heel that has crushed it.
Mark Twain

August 1

Rejoice (*Phillipians 4:4-9*)

Thought for Today: "Finally, my brothers, rejoice in the Lord!" (*Philippians 3:1*)

"Mom, you'd make Christianity more appealing if you were cheerful," our teenage daughter said.

I was hurt and about to reply that it was hard to be cheerful when she acted as she did. But I realized that there was truth in what she had said.

Christians ought to be cheerful always, because we have our Lord, Jesus Christ.

Paul was in prison at the time he wrote Philippians; yet the message coming through the whole book is one of joy through tribulation.

Paul instructs us, "Do not be anxious about anything" (*Philippians 4:6*) but to make our requests known to God through prayer and supplication. Then God will give us peace beyond comprehension.

Prayer: Dear Lord, help us to put all things in your hands and claim your peace. In Jesus' name, Amen. *Dorien K. Miles*

August 2

How to be Happy Throughout the Year

Keep your heart free from hate, Your mind free from worry.
Live simply, expect little, give much.
Sing often, pray always, fill your heart with love.

Scatter sunshine, forget self, think of others.
Do as you would be done by.
These are the tried links in contentment's golden chain.
(*Billy's* favorite)

August 3 **

Thank you, Lord

I cannot thank you Lord enough
For all you've given me,
For your food and shelter, and for love
Of friends and family.
In time of sorrow you stood by
And held my trembling hand,
You wiped the tear drops from my eyes
And helped me to understand.
Although I cannot ever know
What the future has in store,
Your love will always see me through,
'Til we meet on paradise shore.
Elsie Natalie Brady

August 4

Smell the Roses

Slow down and smell the roses
On your busy, active day.
Slow down and breathe their fragrance,,

Where they grow along life's way.
Take a minute of your lifetime
To enjoy a pretty bloom.
Pick a rose from nature's garden,
It will brighten up your room.
Be not haste in all your doings
As you hurry through the day,
But enjoy what God gives freely;
Smell the roses while you may.
Bill Carr

August 5

A Sense of Purpose

The quality of life can be enhanced dramatically by a sincere belief in God and willingness to serve Him according to Canon R. C. Stephens

"Does religion really make a difference to one's life?" is a question often asked in these cynical days, for some people feel that they are getting along well enough without having any religious allegiance.

Yet religion can bring a great joy and sense of purpose to life, though it depends, of course, to a great extent on what *sort* of religion we have and how real our faith is to us.

The religion of many of the people in our Lord's time was irrational: the gods they worshipped were often capricious and vindictive. The Pharisees seemed to be more concerned with outward respectability than inward integrity. But Christianity, with its emphasis on love as the key to happiness is ethically one of the noblest world religions.

Looking back through the history of the Western world we find that those who have contributed most to the welfare of their fellow men have had the guidance and strength of the Christian Faith to help them.

The difference referred to in the original question is seen most clearly in those who are convinced that "all things are naked and opened unto the eyes of Him with whom we have to do." (*Hebrews 4:13*). For we can test ourselves by studying our attitude to our work or daily chores. "He that is faithful in that which is least is faithful also in much." (*Luke 16:10*).

Too many today are content with what will "pass muster", too few are concerned with giving value for money, feeling no compulsion to serve God by the honest service of their fellow men. But the diligent Christian workman has no need to feel ashamed. He tries to do all to the glory of God.

I am reminded of the story of one of the old cathedral builders in the ages of faith. The King expostulated with a monk who was carving a beautiful angel in a dark recess where it would hardly ever be noticed. "Sire," replied the monk, "God can see in the dark corners." It is that sort of faith and conviction which comes out unmistakably in what we are and what we do, and which makes a very great difference to our lives.

Aug 6

The Ship of Life

Take my hand and help me through
The journey of this day –
Guide my thoughts and show me what
You would have me say.

Lift me up when I oft fall
Help me when I fail –
Place me in the eye of the storm
As I walk through the gale.

August 7 *

May the Lord of peace be gracious
And reach out to you this day
With His many special blessings,
And the love He sends your way.

August 8

You are my Leaning Post

You are my leaning post, dear Lord,
My shelter and my rock.
You open up the door to me
Each time You hear me knock.
All I need to do is ask
And you provide the way.
You hear me when I call to You
The times I kneel to pray.
Thank you, Lord, for Your great love,
Your comfort and Your care.
It's such a joy for me to know
I may seek and find You there.
Jean Conder Soule

August 9

When day is done and shadows fall
And the night seems dark and long,
Worry not then O, child of God
Sleep, for soon cometh the dawn.
His love endures forevermore
There never was such a friend,
Thus, he stands so eager to help
With courage right to the end.
No, God's never beyond our reach
He's only a prayer away,
Trust Him always, look to His love
He's watching and waiting today.
Mary E. Harrington

August 10

Open Your Heart to Jesus

Open up your heart to Jesus –
Let His Spirit enter in –
And forever, be your Savior
From life's struggles and their sins;
Let Him be your true companion,
On each road you've chosen to trod,
And be your guide to Christian glories
On this earth and unto God.
Open up your heart – and heartaches –
To His mercy and His care
And be blessed with saving graces

In your life and in your prayers;
He is waiting to endure you,
With the love that He imparts,
When you open up the shutters
To the closets in your heart.
Michael Dubina

August 11 *

The Bible says:

"All the scripture is given
by inspiration of God,
and is profitable
for doctrine, for reproof,
for correction,
for instruction in righteousness."
(*2 Timothy 3:16*)

August 12

The Power of God

He gives me faith within myself
When it seems all in vain.
He gives me hope to battle on
And help my goals attain.
He gives me faith and inner strength.

August 13

A Purpose in All Things

Although we may sometimes become discouraged when our efforts seem wasted, God often turns these defeats into victories, Rev. Dr. David M. Owens tells us

Many people believe that Jesus may have given his parable of the Sower (Mark 4:1-8) to his disciples in response to the discouragement they were feeling. Perhaps they had asked him why so much of their effort seemed to be yielding so few results, and he wanted to reassure them that, in spite of wasted seed, in the end the harvest was sure.

Today we often raise this same question of life's apparent wastage. We look at the world we live in and wonder why so much of it should be uninhabitable – too hot, too cold, or too dry. "What a waste!" we may say, but is it?

Hasn't the Creator rather blessed us with a world of contrast and variety? Haven't these "obstacles" also served to bring out the best in man, creating the will to strive and conquer? And when life holds challenges, we are at our best.

We should look at Christian service in the same way, recognizing as a principal of discipleship that everything which happened in the life of Jesus has its counterpart in the life of his disciples. Did anyone sow more seeds of goodness than Jesus? Yet, if success is seen in terms of lasting popularity, then His Ministry seemed a failure. He was led friendless to Calvary and his mission seemed lost. What happened to the crowds who had supported Him? Had all his teaching and healing been in vain?

But looking back, we now know that no life was ever more fruitful. God changed defeat into victory, purposelessness into profit, and it is in that faith that we go about his work in the world.

I visited a man in hospital recently who was awaiting major surgery. He had been ill for several weeks, the first illness of his life, and lying in bed he had time to think. He confessed that he hadn't been to church or given thought to Christian truths since he was a boy. "But lying in bed," he said, "so much has come back to me, especially the things my mother and Sunday School teacher taught me about the Bible, and I am happy to say I have been able to quote verses which have not been on my tongue since those days." Thus, even illness served a purpose, as did the goodly influence he had known so long ago in childhood.

Take heart, for what may look at first like waste and fruitlessness may turn out to be part of God's harvest.

August 14 *

God's Stairway

Step by step we climb day by day
Closer to God with each prayer we pray.
For the "cry of the heart" offered in prayer
Becomes just another *spiritual stair*
In the *heavenly staircase* leading us to
A beautiful place where we live anew ...
So never give up for it's worth the climb
To live forever in endless time
Where the soul of man is *safe and free*
To live in love through eternity!

August 15

Forgiveness is the fragrance a violet sheds
on the heel that has crushed it.
Mark Twain

August 16 *

You're Not Alone

You're not alone when troubles come
and your heart is beating like a drum.
You're not alone through sorrow's night
when nothing seems to go just right.
The Savior waits to hear from you
and give you strength for all you do.
He knows the secrets of your heart,
and he can make your fears depart.
You're not alone without a guide –
He sees each tear you've ever cried.
You're not alone for Christ is there.
God comforts those who seek His way
and knows our hearts before we pray.
His perfect peace and endless love
fall like feathers from above.
There is no cross too large to bear –
You're not alone for Christ is there!
Clay Harrison

August 17

Feelings

I love to feel
The sun upon my back,
A breeze upon my face,
A joy within my heart
That nothing can erase.
I wait to feel each season
That God will show my way,
To experience each night,
I long to see each day.
The morning bird's sweet song
That sounds so free and clear;
It permeates the air
As an echo does the ear.
When I pray at night,
I thank the Lord above
For the miracles of His hand,
His undying love.

James Joseph Huesgen

August 18

Wings of Faith

On the wings of faith in Jesus,
I am master of each day
That is mine to serve and praise Him
At my labors and my play.

For he guides me in each journey
To embrace the Christian's way
That reward me with His blessings
And needs for which I pray.
On the wings of faith in Jesus
I am safe from earthly harm,
For I am forever guarded
By His care and loving arms,
And I'm never lost or hopeless
In life's traumas and defeats
For my faith and trust in Jesus
Is a Christian faith – complete.
Michael Dubina

August 19 *

My Hand in His

Oh wondrous Savior Who art mine
May my small hand remain in Thine,
That I not independent be
But anchored solely, Lord in Thee!
And Christ, may I in Thee abide
That I not leave Thy wounded side,
But see the sorrows Thou hast bourne
Before the dawn of Easter morn.
Oh blessed Jesus, hear my prayer
That I may ever be aware
Of Thy dear love, which like a balm
Can sin-sick surging souls becalm.
Oh dear and precious Prince of Peace

Whose tender mercy does not cease,
Oh may my life like light so shine
That it be patterned after Thine!
Sancie Earman King

August 20

Faithful Prayer

Let it be a regular part of our lives rather than an appeal for help in tight corners, the Rev. David M. Owen says

In Shakespeare's play, *The Tempest*, the despairing mariners, beaten by raging storms, cry, "All lost! To prayers, to prayers." It has been observed in such sophisticated places as the Universities of Oxford and Cambridge that chapel attendance increases just before important examinations, a tendency characterized by H. G. wells, who confessed that he only prayed in emergencies.

Of course, we should pray in tight corners. When our knees knock, the best thing we can do is kneel on them! But true prayer is more than just a stop-gap remedy and a device for getting what we want. A small boy, when asked if he prayed every night said, "No some nights I don't want anything." This reduces God to a kind of benevolent storekeeper who dispatches goods on request.

True prayer is constantly worshipping and thanking God, confessing our failures and seeking for a deeper faith rather than just making SOS appeals when the need arises. God is not at our beck and call to be sought when we want Him, and dispensed when we don't. Since we are answerable ultimately to

Him, then He truly is the last resort, but primarily He is the first resort.

When astronaut John Glenn was asked by the Press if he had made any special prayers for God's protection while in outer space, he replied that his religion was so much a part of his day-to-day life that he found it unnecessary to make emergency prayers for God's protection at times of special need. We would all do well to heed that sound bit of spiritual advice.

Prayer for the week: Lord, make my prayers as faithful as your constant love.

August 21

God is Near

No matter how steep your mountain,
The Lord will climb it with you.
He will light your path in darkness,
His hand will guide you through.
There is really nothing
In this vast world to fear.
God hears all of your questions,
He sends the answers so clear.
"Have faith, My child," He teaches us,
In the stars that shine at night.
Believe in Christ, your Savior.
Your world will be all right.
Edna Louise Gilbert

August 22 *

Our Heavenly Father, it is your glory always to have grace and mercy. Bring back all who have erred and strayed from your ways; continue to lead us all to embrace in faith the Truth of your Word and to hold it fast. Now and forevermore. Amen.

August 23 *

May He fill your heart with gladness –
May he hear your every prayer
And be there to keep you always
In His warm and gentle care.

August 24

Count your blessings instead of your crosses,
Count your gains instead of your losses,
Count your joys instead of your woes,
Count your friends instead of your foes,
Count your full years instead of your lean,
Count your kind deeds instead of your mean,
Count your courage instead of your fears,
Count your health instead of your wealth.

August 25

Home may be a simple shanty
Beneath the stars above,
But blessed be those who dwell within
A house that is built with love!
Clay Harrison

August 26

Prayer: Dear God, I do not always understand your ways, but help me accept your wisdom with unquestioning trust; in Jesus, Amen.
Sudha Khristmukti

August 27

Ask for what you want, but be willing to take what God gives you. It may be better than what you ask.
Norman Vincent Peale

August 28

Be sure to remember that nothing in
Your daily life is so insignificant and so
Inconsequential that the Lord will not help
You by answering your prayer.
O. Hallesby

August 29

In Name Only

Many people call themselves Christians but do not live according to the Bible, says Canon R. C. Stephens

Nowadays, all the bottles, boxes and packets we see around in the shops, have to have the contents plainly stated on them so that we know just what we are buying.

However, labeling is not confined to things; many people insist on labeling people – often incorrectly. A brief encounter, a casual conversation or a chance remark can be sufficient to form a wrong opinion of others and an adjective, such as mean or uncharitable, may be attached to them forever more. Greater knowledge might change such ideas, but all too frequently little trouble is taken to put right those false impressions and, in this way, reputations have suffered.

This sort of thing has been going on for centuries; the first followers of Jesus soon collected a label and became known as people "who followed the new way" (*Acts 9:2*). Their enemies didn't like what they said or what they did, so they plotted to get rid of them. Persecution led by Saul (*later to be St. Paul*) broke out in Jerusalem and he received permission from the high priest to arrest and imprison the disciples. Many, however, escaped and some eventually reached Antioch three hundred miles to the north where, after Saul's conversion, they received another name, probably as a nickname – "Christians" (*Acts 11:26*) and it has stuck to them ever since.

It would have been very easy for those early Christians to have hidden themselves away and no one would have ever known about them, but the love within them, even for those who hated them, prevented this. They wanted others to share their joy and their conviction of a life after this because Jesus rose from the dead, and consequently many of them paid the penalty for that love.

We bear the same name label as those first Christians, but do we show in our lives the same spirit of Jesus or are we content to be Christians in name only?

August 30

Petition in Faith

When your problems rise up
To bog and depress,
And your spirit gives way to despair;
When your mind is a vent
To a burden's intent,
And your lips can't give voice to prayer –
Turn away from the thoughts
That cause you distress,
They hinder the self in repair;
Trust God to provide
What the heartstrings confide;
With assurance, you're still in His care.
Roxie Lusk Smith

August 31

The Good Shepherd

The Lord is my Shepherd
And I am His lamb;
He keeps watch over me
Wherever I am.
He leads me to pastures
Where all is serene;
Beside still waters of prayer;
My sins are washed clean.
Should I stray from the fold
On pathways unknown,
He leaves the ninety-nine
And carries me home.

September

Lord, I give You my fears,
Give me Your strength.

September 1

The Eye of the Needle (*Luke 18:21-27*)

In times of Jesus, towns and cities were surrounded by walls. Entrances were often formed by a tunnel-like arch that could be walled off in the event of an attack. The tunnel was often called "the eye of the needle," for it was a small opening that could not easily be found. In order for camels to enter such a tunnel, they had to kneel. The animals had to be led through the darkness and were often stripped of any trappings that would require extra space. A camel being asked to crawl is about as cooperative as a mule.

So it is, God says, with a wealthy person. All arrogant trappings must be removed as the person kneels to God's leadership. Even though humans can be more stubborn than camels or mules, still it is possible for God to lead them through the tunnels of life.

September 2

God Grant Us Faith, Hope and Love

Hope for a world grown cynically cold
Hungry for Power and greedy for gold ...
Faith to believe when within and without
There's a nameless fear in a world of doubt ...
Love that is bigger than race or creed,
To cover the world and fulfill each need ...
God, grant these gifts of Faith, Hope and Love –
Three things this world has so little of ...

For only these gifts from our Father above
Can turn man's sins from hatred to Love.

September 3 *

Lord, thank You for another day
within this life of mine
Give me the strength to live it well,
whatever I may find.
Bestow from Your abundance
whatever I may lack.
To use the hours wisely,
for I cannot have them back.
Lord, thank You for another day,
in which to make amends.
For slights or petty words,
inflicted on my friends.
For sometimes losing patience
with problems that I find.
For seeing faults in other lives,
but not the ones in mine.
Lord, thank you for another chance,
in which to try to be
a little more deserving
of the gifts You've given me.
For yesterday is over,
and tomorrow's far away,
and I remain committed
to the good I do today!

September 4

Meetings with God

We may meet God anywhere, explains Canon R. C. Stephens, so we should take care that we do not pass Him by

In coming to save the world, Christ gave a vision of God which has attracted men and women to His service ever since. Throughout His ministry thousands flocked to see Him, not only to hear what He said, but because He gave them a picture of what God is like. Zacchaeus, the tax collector, climbed a tree in order to see Him and Christ's presence had a profound effect on him, so that his way of life was changed and he returned what he had wrongfully taken from others (*Luke 19:8*): he became a new person.

Spiritual progress depends on the use we make of moments when we realize that God is near, for the clearer our idea of God, the clearer our knowledge of ourselves. Isaiah and St. Paul both became more alive after their spiritual encounters, and St. Paul could still say after many years. "I was not disobedient unto the heavenly vision" (*Acts 26:19*).

Many Christians may say this sort of thing is not for them; they are just ordinary people and expressions of visions and spiritual experiences seem extravagant religious jargon. But God's revelation is not confined to the mystical and strange. God is also the God of the commonplace and reveals Himself in the normal activities of people, and we recognize these everyday incidents for what they are – meetings with God – otherwise they will pass us by unnoticed.

Whenever we have been moved by a text or have been uplifted by music, art, or beauty of the natural world, this is His visitation, and as such is as real and valid as any mystical experience of the saints. It gives vitality to our resolutions to overcome temptations and brings peace in the midst of sorrow and strength in our service for God. Let us then be alert with open hearts and minds to recognize and welcome His coming.

September 5

You Life Will be Blest if You Look for the Best

It's easy to grow downhearted
when nothing goes your way,
It's easy to be discouraged
when you have a troublesome day,
But trouble is only a challenge
to spur you on to achieve
The Best that God has to offer
if you have the Faith to Believe.

September 6 *

Lead Thou the Way

Each time I speak, let what I say
Be of Thy Word,
That those who listen shall be blessed
For having heard.
Of what I do let every move
Be first of prayer,
That in touch of other hearts
I shall not err.

And when I walk my feet shall take
Thy chosen way,
That those who hold my hand shall not
Be led astray!
Esther Nilsson

September 7

God Knows Best

God knows best in everything,
Though we can't always understand
Why things don't work out
Exactly as we've planned.
For He knows when it is time to bring
The sunshine or the rain,
And an always cheerful rainbow
To alleviate our pain.
So always look to God above
When your soul is needing rest,
And you will soon be comforted
By knowing He knows best.
Rachel Hartnett

September 8

Being Aware

God never deserts us, but it is up to us to recognize Him and listen to His voice, explains Canon R. C. Stephens

When people worshiped heathen gods, they brought presents or offered sacrifices, even their own children (*Jeremiah 32:35*), in an attempt to obtain their requests.

But God is not like that at all. He doesn't wait for us to approach Him, neither does He require gifts to make Him attentive: He contacts us and doesn't limit His presence to those who believe in Him. Jacob was not a religious person, nor particularly good, but he needed help after he wronged his brother, so God came while he slept, blessing him and promising to be with him (*Genesis 28:15*).

An even more remarkable instance shows that God's initiative is not limited to His own people, when he stirred up the spirit of Cyrus, King of Persia" (*about 536 BC*) to see that captive Jews returned to rebuild the temple at Jerusalem (*2 Corinthians 36:22-23*). The greatest intervention into human affairs was the coming of Jesus, proving that God is not only interested in the great events of history but in the everyday life of the individual.

But many still act as if the first move towards God must be made by them. In a play, a prompter is at the side of the stage to help the actors who forget their lines, but the actors may ignore the prompt. God is in 'the wings' of life to prompt us to do what is right – we may ignore His voice or our minds may be so cluttered with important matters we simply do not hear what He has to say.

Rae Snowden Martin

However, He doesn't give up, but 'nudges' us to remind us of His presence and 'jogs' our memories to recall those occasions when He sustained and comforted us and in times of joy, enhanced our happiness. Let us not be like the two disciples on the Emmaus road who, when "Jesus Himself drew near", failed to recognize Him.

September 9 *

Thank God for Little Things

Thank You, God, for little things
that often come our way –
Things we take for granted
but don't mention when we pray –
The unexpected courtesy,
the thoughtful, kindly deed –
A hand reached out to help us
in the time of need –
Oh make us more aware, dear God,
of little daily graces
That come to us with "sweet surprise"
from never-dreamed of places.

September 10

The Long Way Around

In following our faith, we should expect the path to be a long and circuitous one, explains Canon R.C. Stephens

At school, I was taught that a straight line was the shortest distance between two points and on a map. It certainly is. But, since the earth is round, the shortest distance between two places is not a straight line but a curve, and a navigator crosses the oceans by using what are known as 'great circles'.

This is what God seemed to do when He brought the Jews out of captivity in Egypt. He had already decided the destination He had for them – the Promised Land – but instead of leading them through the land of the Philistines, which was the obvious route (*Exodus 13:17*). He took them through the wilderness for forty years. Had they gone directly through Canaan, few, if any, would have survived, for as freed slaves they would not have been a match for their well-equipped, organized enemies. Time was needed to weld them into a united people and what happened to be the longest way around proved to be the best for them.

Most of us at some time have been led astray by taking the so-called short-cut and have found ourselves lost. With people the direct approach is not always fruitful, for a straight attack can harden the resistance of the heart and mind against accepting or absorbing new truths and ideas. Had Jesus applied the method to Nicodemus, I don't think the ruler would have listened or responded, but Christ's more indirect way immediately captured his interest – it proved to be a roundabout course but he was won around in the end.

There is no short-cut to learning, and certainly not in Christian discipleship. For most of us a long journey lies ahead, often a circuitous route, but if we plod along faithfully we shall arrive. Most people want to find happiness in their Christian living, yet if they seek it for themselves it will elude them. Only by the oblique way of making others happy and serving them for Christ's sake will they find joy.

September 11

A Guide That Never Falters

There is a guide that never falters
Amidst the storms of doubts and fears,
For He has walked the way before thee,
And He knows the path you see;
His feet have trod the rugged hillsides,
And the valleys of despair –
His life has paved the way to heaven,
Never fear, He'll guide you there;
His soul has tasted moral anguish,
His eyes have felt the sting of tears,
He's a timely guide, a sympathetic Savior,
So, trust Him in your future years.
Elizabeth E. S. Williams

September 12 *

You Never Walk Alone

You never walk alone my friend
Though you may think you do,
For in your sorrow and despair
God always walks with you.
There is no hour, no passing day,
He is not by your side,
And though unseen He still is there
To be your friend and guide
Whene'er you think you are alone
Reach out and you will find,
The hand of God to show the way
And bring you peace of mind.
Harold F. Mohn

September 13

For Our Own Good

God can show us His love and we hope we can follow Him, but the final decision has to be ours, says Canon R. C. Stephens

As a child I hated being ordered to do anything, even though it was for my own good, but now I sometimes wish that I didn't have to take any responsibility and so be relieved of worry and temptation. From the beginning of creation, God has never forced anyone to do anything, but He suffers when He sees us going away from Him. He outlined the way for us to follow and sent Jesus as His example of "the Way" (*John 14:6*), hoping that we might recognize how wonderful Christianity is. He offers all the help we require but He will not wrap us in cotton wool to keep us from harm, neither will He do for us what we are quite capable of doing ourselves. St. Paul pointed out that we are to work out "our own salvation" (*Philippians 2:12*).

In the parable of the talents (*Matthew 25:14-30*), the servants were left some money without any definite instructions on what they were supposed to do – the master left that to their own initiative. All three were given the opportunity of developing as people and breaking free from the slave mentality of only doing what they were told. The servant who had only one talent was reprimanded because he failed to do anything at all with his master's money.

It seems that God has put us on earth as a training ground to see how we use His material gifts, for our characters develop by the way we use them. We can use them for the benefit of others, but we cannot stand aside and do nothing. Christ showed how important a matter this was when He said, "If, then, you have not proved trustworthy with the wealth of this world, who will trust you with the wealth that is real – in the next? (*Luke 16:11*).

September 14

Not to Seek, Lord, but to Share

Dear God, much too often
we seek You in prayer
Because we are wallowing
in our own self-despair ...
We make every word

we lamentingly speak
An imperative plea
for whatever we seek ...
We pray for ourselves
and seldom for others,
We're concerned with our problems
and not with our brothers ...
We seem to forget, Lord,
that the "sweet hour of prayer"
Is not for self-seeking
but to place in Your care ...
All the lost souls
unloved and unknown
And to keep praying for them
until they're your own ...
For it's never enough
to seek God in prayer
With no thought of others
who are in despair ...
So teach us, dear God,
That the power of prayer
Is made stronger by placing
the world in Your Care!

September 15

Freedom does not mean you can do what you please,
but it does mean that there isn't anything holding you back
from striving to make your finest dreams come true.

# # #

Thoughtfulness is to friendship as
Sunshine is to a garden.

September 16

God's Purpose

In times of suffering we should remember that God is there to help us, says Canon R. C. Stephens

The natural disasters which occur from time to time prevent many from believing in a loving God. If the created world was good (*Genesis 1:31*), why do so many have to suffer from tidal waves and earthquakes? But God's creation is living, "the ceaseless round of circling planets singing on their way", and it continues to develop and change. The earth as it was "in the beginning" is very different today – for instance, the chalk hills and sand beds of Surrey were under the sea millions of years ago. St. Paul wrote with great insight, "For we know that the whole creation groaneth and travaileth in pain together until now" (*Romans 8:22*) indicating that the universe is working towards perfection.

Another stumbling block to belief is the scourge of disease, such as cancer. Why should men, women and children suffer from this? Medical researchers are now conquering these dread illnesses, as they did years ago against tuberculosis and diptheria, and in their victories "God is working His purposes out".

We are inconsistent in our approach to life if we ask for protection from pain and tragedy: parents don't wrap their children in cotton wool to prevent them from accidents, or stop them from rock climbing and other dangerous activities. They let them take their chance so that they can develop naturally. So, God has put us in a world of high risk – a risk which mankind has greatly increased by his inventions and foolishness.

Some look on Christianity as an insurance policy to preserve them from calamities; but no commercial company would promise that, only compensation after an accident. When terrible and tragic things happen to us and our loved ones, God in His love and compassion compensates us by reconstituting our lives, providing we allow Him to do so, picking us up when we are broken, then strengthening us and recreating us for his purpose.

September 17 *

Nobody Walks Alone

Oft' times when the highway of life seems rough
And all of your dreams have flown,
Just remember, wherever your road may go,
Nobody walks alone.
When everyone else has let you down
And under your sins you groan,
Just keep reminding your burdened heart,
Nobody walks alone.
Then suddenly you'll feel His hand in yours,
And His eyes lifting up your own,
And you'll hear His gentle, forgiving voice:
"Nobody walks alone" ...
Nick Kenny

September 18

Faith Dispels Fear

This week the Rev. David M. Owen suggests that when troubled by fears, we need to remember that we are surrounded by the love of God

When Winston Churchill and President Roosevelt met during the Second World War to formulate the Atlantic Charter, they stated the Four Freedoms to which they believed all people were entitled. One of these is the Freedom from Fear. They were thinking, of course, of the fears induced by and resulting from power politics, affecting race and creed.

These fears and many more are still with us today, awaiting a solution by the world's governments, but there are other fears that lie outside the jurisdiction of politics – the personal fears of illness and pain, fears of our relationships with other people going wrong, fears of loneliness, of death.

My job as a clergyman enables me to meet people with all sorts of fears. I certainly find that all sorts of fears are excusable and need a great deal of pastoral concern, but I am also confronted with other fears that are unnecessary and ill-founded.

I wonder sometimes if our fears are not a bit like those of Don Quixote blindfolded and hung by his wrists from a stable window, he was told that a great abyss yawned beneath him. But, as he cringed in terror of the fall, Maritones cut the cord that held him, and he fell just four inches!

The Bible tells us that the fear of the Lord is the beginning of knowledge (*Proverbs 1:7*). This does not, of course, mean that we are to be frightened of God, but rather that we are to fear more those things that separate us from Him and prevent us enjoying the life He has given. It is when we stand in awe of Him as one who "holds the whole world in His hands", and yet we know Him to be our Father, that we find faith, joy and peace, that those fears with which we have been burdened are either dispelled or assume much smaller proportions.

Prayer for the week: Lord I give you my fears: give me your strength.

September 19

No Favor do I Seek Today

I come not to ask, to plead or implore You,
I come just to tell You how much I adore You,
For to kneel in Your presence makes me feel blest
And it fills me with joy just to linger with You.
As my soul You replenish and my heart You renew,
For prayer is much more than just asking for things –
It's the peace and contentment that quietness brings ...
So, thank You again for Your mercy and love
And for making me heir to Your Kingdom above!

September 20

Christ's Faithful Soldiers

We are soldiers in the battle for Christianity, and we must not desert our post, says Canon R. C. Stephens

It was very fortunate for Christianity that St. Paul discovered his new found faith was not a philosophy but a battle. Military terms are found in almost every letter he wrote, showing the importance of the battle. He was familiar with Roman soldiers and their equipment, even naming parts of their armor. I suppose if he was writing today he would say something like: "Put on your bullet-proof vest of righteousness, and your steel helmet of salvation, and your automatic gun of the spirit, which is the word of God."

Timothy was to "war good warfare" (*1 Timothy 1:18*) and Paul used expressions such as "fellow soldier", "armor of light" and "fight against the tricks of the devil". Many of us have been baptized with the words, "not to be ashamed to confess the faith of Christ crucified and manually to fight ... and continue as Christ's faithful soldier." But some have forgotten their commission and become soft or deserted.

Christians today are not led to understand that they have entered a war. It is only personal temptation which has to be fought, it is evil and wrong in every way. We may think we can do little, but each victory, however small, is a victory for Christ. In most battles we do not know which side is going to win, but in Christian warfare we can be certain who will win – Christ. As the hymn says, "Who in the strength of Jesus's trust is more than conqueror."

Some may say that evil or wickedness do triumph sometimes, and that is true – because we think we can conquer in our own strength. St. Paul said we were to "Put on the armor of God" (*Ephesians 6:11*). In the last century Canon Pusey said, "Whenever I am tempted to do wrong and need Christ's strength, I make the sign of the cross as a silent prayer and Jesus conquered for me – I have never known it to fail."

At the sign of triumph, Satan's host doth flee: On then, Christian soldiers, on to victory.

September 21

Faith is confident assurance
concerning what we hope for,
and conviction about things
we do not see.
(*Hebrews 11:1*)

September 22

Faith is not a blind leap in the dark
but a surrender to
the goodness and wisdom of God.

##

A memory is a treasure that survives.

September 23

The Perfect Gift

We live and learn in this old world
And as we older grow,
Still more and more we realize,
It's so little that we know.
There is one thing that we wish we knew,
It's where and when to speak
And how to say the things we feel
To help the poor and weak.

So many times we want to talk,
But don't know what to say,
To give someone the strength he needs
To help him on his way.
If God would grant one perfect gift,
To one so small and weak,
The thing I'd ask is just to know
When, where and how to speak.
Laina Owen

September 24

I Cannot Change the World

I cannot change the world, Lord,
No matter how I try.
Only You have power
Of things beneath the sky.
But, still You do encourage
The little things I do,
Like showing love and kindness
And telling folks of You.
I cannot change the world, Lord,
But I can love and care.
I know that You will nurture
Each seed I plant out there.
And You will bring forth blossoms
From little things I do.
I cannot change the world, Lord,
But I'll do my best for You.
John and Edna Massimilla

September 25

Breaking our Chains

The liberty which Christ offers can be ours, if we are willing to accept it, explains Canon R. C. Stephens

One of the most exciting themes in the Bible is God's message of release from bondage – a bondage which began when Adam and Eve disobeyed Him in the Garden of Eden – but it is also the story of those who preferred to remain in captivity.

The Hebrews in Egypt were slaves until God marched them out under Moses. Not all the people approved: some lost their desire for freedom at the first sign of danger and wanted to return to Egypt; others complained that God provided manna for them to eat and looked back longingly to the varied diet they had enjoyed as slaves (*Numbers 11: 5-6*). Even when they were brought to the very borders of Canaan and found that it was a land "flowing of milk and honey" as God had promised, they were afraid of the inhabitants and refused to enter (*Numbers 13:17-33*). God had to wait until a new generation had grown up to possess the land.

Christ's first sermon in the synagogue at Nazareth proclaimed "deliverance to the captives" – He freed men and women from physical and spiritual bondage – the man paralyzed physically by sin (*Luke 5: 13:18-25*) and the woman "whom Satan hath bound, lo, these eighteen years" was made straight (*Luke 13:11-14*). But not everyone accepted the liberty which Christ offered. A young man who was tied to his riches and was told to sell all that he had and follow Jesus went away "sorrowful" because he couldn't break away from his possessions.

People can become slaves to almost anything: a person can be tied to his or her work to such an extent that family relationships suffer; others have a drinking problem from which they say they could break free whenever they wish and will not admit that they cannot. Chains are only broken with God's help and the staunch friends He sends us, but the first essential is to *want* to be free – only then can He help us to experience "the glorious liberty of the children of God" (*Romans 8:21*).

September 26

My Heart's Prayer

In the dawning of this new year,
It brings such joy within
To see where You have brought me Lord –
From places where I've been.
You always walk beside me, Lord.
You dry my every tear.
You light the path before me.
You chase away my fears.
Each day is such a precious gift.
Oh, may I live each day
So full of joy and purpose,
As you guide me on life's way.
Mary Ann Jameson

September 27

Know Thyself

Christ helps us both to know ourselves and to seek forgiveness for our sins, explains Canon R. C. Stephens

Although we hear a great deal about forgiveness, very few people really want it, because they don't seriously believe that there is anything to be forgiven. They know they aren't thieves or terrorists and are free from grosser sins. Yet the subject of forgiveness figures prominently in the Gospels, and Scripture classes everyone as sinners.

The man sick of the palsy came to be healed and was healed and was told, "thy sins be forgiven thee," for Jesus saw the man's need of forgiveness if he was to remain cured. St. John was aware of this blindness to our true condition when he wrote, "If we say that we have no sin, we deceive ourselves and the truth is not in us (*1 John 1:8*). That's just it, we *do* deceive ourselves, and either refuse to take our shortcomings seriously, or to even acknowledge that we have any.

The scribes and Pharisees, for example, didn't believe that they were sinners and so came in for Christ's criticism. They wanted others to think how good and generous they were, and showed off in public (*Matthew 6:2,5*), but in private they were lacking in mercy and faith.

It may seem strange that anyone should try to act in such a hypocritical way, but, it is a common fault today. Many people behave charmingly with strangers but are thoroughly selfish at home and think nothing of it.

Part of Christ's work was to show people themselves – what they are really like – and then He could help them. This happened with the palsied man mentioned above, and also with the heathen woman from Canaan who made out that she was a believer and flatteringly began, "O Lord, Thou Son of David..." (*Matthew 15:22*). Jesus took no notice of her until she put aside all pretense and then her request was granted.

Philosophers of old used to say, "Know thyself", and Christ assists us to do this. When we honestly know ourselves, we recognize that we need forgiveness, and we also discover that until we are forgiven, our Lord can do little for us.

September 28 *

Lord Speak to Me

Lord, speak to me in such a way
That I may surely know –
The purpose that You have for me;
The path that I must go.
Then, when the pathway is made clear,
And the journey I begin,
When fear and doubt start creeping in –
Please speak to me again.
Remind me of Your presence, Lord,
Each mile along the way.
Let not my steps grow weary –
Keep speaking, lest I stray.
The roadblocks will be many,
Dead ends I'm sure to see;
But, I'll reach my destination, Lord,
Because You spoke to me.
D. Sue (Jones) Horton

September 29

Serenity Prayer

God, grant me serenity
to accept things I cannot change;
Courage to change things I can;
And wisdom to know the difference.

September 30

The essence of courage is not
that your heart should not quake
but that nobody else should know.
E. F. Benson

###

Believe, dream, will ...
and put it in the hands of God.
Norman Vincent Peale

October

Pray for a good harvest,
but continue to hoe.

October 1

Break into Usefulness

When Christ breaks into our hearts, life can never be the same again, says Canon R. C. Stephens

When things are broken, we generally consider them to be useless, but not always. Some only fulfill their purpose when they are broken. An egg shell must be smashed to let the chick escape from its prison; a horse is broken in so that its strength is used efficiently and no one except a scientist could ever have discovered the enormous power released in the splitting of the atom.

The crowds which followed Jesus were conscious not only of a wonderful preacher and an attractive personality but also of His strength. He spoke with authority which made them listen; they saw His miracles when He conquered disease; His word controlled the forces of nature – "He commandeth even the winds and water, and they obey Him" (*Luke 8:25*) – and the devils were subject to Him. He broke the five loaves creating sufficient for the multitude. But there was also power within Himself to be freed – He prophesied, "I, if I be lifted up from the earth, will draw all men unto Me" (*John 12:32*). When His body was broken on the cross it was released, and since then the lives of many have been changed by Him.

Hosea once said, "break up your fallow ground" (*Hosea 10:12*), referring to the land which turns hard when unused. It reminded me of Christ's parable, the Sower, and the ground which had been trodden underfoot (the wayside) – had the surface been broken up the seed would have taken root and brought forth fruit. Some lives are like that hard ground – their spirits lie dormant and little that is spiritual can develop in them until Christ comes. He always takes the initiative, yet He will not force entrance into our lives. But give Him the slightest encouragement and He will break in to free our spirits and allow spiritual desires to grow. Sometimes His coming is almost violent, at other times He enters secretly into our hearts, but in either case the result is the same – life is changed and can never be the same again because He has drawn us to Himself.

October 2

Their Master's Voice

Old dogs seem to take it in stride
the passing of each day,
Content to let the hours pass
whatever comes their way.
They seem to know a secret
which offers peace of mind –
A secret dogs just seem to know,
and humans seldom find.
They lead an unassuming life
and know their master's voice.
A simple touch of their master's hand
will cause them to rejoice.
They listen for his footsteps
and wait beside the door,
Content to let the world go by
to serve him evermore.

If only humans had such faith
to seek the Master's voice
Content to let the world go by –
to worship and rejoice!
Clay Harrison

October 3

Remembering to Pray

"Ask and it shall be given,"
So the Lord would have you pray.
"Seek and you will surely find,"
For He will show the way.
"Knock and it shall be opened."
Do you think God is about
To turn His back on us,
Knowing all we are without?
We are His little children,
In this valley full of tears,
We need His love to guide us,
And give meaning to the years.
To cross life's troubled waters,
There is not a better way,
Than in clinging to Him tightly,
And remembering to pray.
Grace E. Easley

October 4

Doing Things Your Way

I wonder what your plans are, Lord.
How will I live this day?
I pray that I can please You
In each and every way.
I hope to be kind and helpful
To everyone that I see.
Let joy and love shine from my heart
So they may see You through me.
I pray that I can help others
Through their periods of pain and sorrow.
Let me help them find hope and peace
Until they have a brighter tomorrow.
Our time on earth is, oh, so short,
It's just a passing through;
So let me be your instrument
In the things that You would do.
If I can be a source of comfort
To one saddened soul today
And help to spread Your wisdom,
Then I am doing things Your way.

Shirley Hile Powell

October 5 *

Psalm 23 (*Paraphrased*)

My God is my overseer and protector,
who makes available to me all I need.
He provides a peaceful environment where I
can go and find relief from the stresses of living.
There I can find a renewal of my spirit that
will enable me to cope with the darkest
and most despairing events of life.
He makes abundant provision for me when
the troubles of life overwhelm me.
He enables me to share in the good things of
the Spirit till the end of my time on earth and beyond.
Evert G. Israelson

October 6

God's Invitations

Although we may be familiar with the words of Jesus' teachings, explains Canon R. C. Stephens, we often fail to make the effort truly to understand them

One of the most difficult verses in the gospels is: "Unto you is given to know the mystery of the kingdom of God; but unto them that are without, all these things are done in parables: that seeing they may see, and not perceive; and hearing they may hear, and not understand" (*Mark 4:11,12*). It seems incredible that Jesus should teach deliberately so that some would not understand. But his decision to teach in parables was taken after His enemies, the Pharisees and the Herodians, plotted to destroy Him (*Mark 3:6*).

He realized that if His enemies were successful, the whole purpose of His coming to earth would prematurely end. By teaching in parables, He could teach His followers, and at the same time His opponents would hear but not understand, and He would avoid arrest. Towards the end of His ministry, His stories were sometimes pointedly against the Pharisees (*Mark 12:12*), but by then His work was practically completed.

That was a long time ago, but I feel that this difficult verse applies today in a different way, not to Christ's enemies but to those who call themselves Christians. Because we know the parables so well, we often fail to understand deeply enough to make us practice what Jesus taught. And this is a particular danger if we know our Bibles well – we do not take in what we hear or read.

If its familiar words are to affect us, we must concentrate and not allow the words to pass over us. For instance, we know the lesson of the Good Samaritan story, and therefore we should not pass by, as we sometimes do, those opportunities of neighborliness because they seem so ordinary and insignificant. The pearl merchant sold everything to buy the one of "great price" (Matthew 13:46). Are we prepared to make sacrifices for what we believe? We consider that the guests were very rude to reject their invitations (Luke 14: 15-24). How many of God's invitations have we refused?

Scripture brings us strength and comfort; let us not allow familiarity to dull our attention so that we hear and not understand, see and not perceive.

October 7

There's More!

God gave us a new name – Christian;
a new family – God's Forever Family
and the privilege of direct access to Him.
We call that prayer.
Prayer is simply communication with God.
In prayer, we can tell God that we
love Him and want to please Him.
In prayer, we can talk to God about our failures
and receive His forgiveness.
In prayer, we can bring all of our needs to God,
and He has promised to provide for us.
In prayer, we can ask God to give His
gift of life to our family, friends,
neighbors, and acquaintances.

October 8

God Bless You and
Keep You in His Care

There are many things in life
That we cannot understand,
But we must trust God's judgement
And be guided by His hand.

And all who have God's blessing
Can rest safely in His care.
For He promises "safe passage"
On the "Wings of Faith and Prayer."

October 9

God will not do the work He has
assigned for you to do.
The impossible is often the untried.

###

Atheist – Someone who has no
invisible means of support.

October 10

Thank You, Lord

I marvel at the splendor that surrounds me,
The beauty that expands from sky to sea.
Oh, God, how can I ever start to thank You
For all the wondrous things You've given me.
I thank You Lord for trees that grace the woodland,
For every growing thing that's bright and fair,
For mountains high and every golden meadow,
For wherever there is beauty You are there.
I see the stars, I feel the sun,
Your majesty spreads far and wide.

I see the light, I feel Your love,
I am safe because You're at my side.
I thank You, Lord, for many countless blessings,
For promises and answers to my prayer.
I never want or fear because You love me,
Dearest Lord, because I know You truly care.
Patience Allison Hartbauer

October 11

Just Look Beyond

Just look beyond today for blessing,
Look past the skies of somber grey,
And look beyond the trials and heartaches
When God will turn night to day.
Dear one, just trust Him in the shadow,
He wants the very best for you.
He'll walk beside you in the valley,
His grace and love will see you through.
Just look beyond today for blessings.
In God's time He'll reveal to you
The many joys that are awaiting,
The joys He's chosen just for you.
So don't give up, keep on believing –
There's happiness ahead for you.
Soon God will turn your trials to triumph,
And skies again will shine bright blue.
Beverly J. Anderson

October 12

The Way to Victory

Inner conflict over our beliefs may go on for years, but the most important thing is never give up the battle, says Canon R. C. Stephens

What a mixture we are – we desire one thing and at the same time we want the opposite. Many people want to have a sylph-like figure yet frequently succumb to the delights of delicious fattening foods; ambition beckons some to strive to be successful but the pleasures of idleness thwart their initiative. We long to be better Christians but there are so many diverse events occupying our lives that it is sometimes difficult to assess their individual merits.

Early in Christ's ministry, Nicodemus went to Jesus to ask Him some questions but little more is heard of him until two or three years later when he helped Joseph at the tomb (*John: 19:39*). In that time gap it seems that a tug-a-war went on inside Nicodemus before he was able to commit himself. I believe this is the experience of many of us who are faced with several choices and take days, months, even years to make up our minds. Perhaps cowardice, lack of faith or fear holds us back – there are all kinds of reasons to prevent us making a decision and we feel a sense of guilt and shame followed by the temptation to give up. It isn't everyone who can settle a matter quickly and irrevocably: St. Paul, even after his conversion, still had to battle between right and wrong and it was years before St. Augustine capitulated to Christ. So, we must take heart and not retreat from the conflict, for that would be to lose the battle. If, on the other hand, we go on fighting we shall go on to victory, for the "man who holds out to the end will be saved" (Matthew 24:13).

October 13

To Keep in Touch

Sometimes I wonder if God thinks
I ask Him for too much.
Forgive me, Lord, for what I feel,
I seem so out of touch.
Oft times I feel a little shy
When problems of the day
Start crowding in upon my mind
And hurt gets in the way.
You know my needs before I ask
When empty that I seem,
You know the way in which I feel,
You share my every dream.
Forgive me, Lord, my doubts and fears
And if I ask too much,
My room is quiet and I can pray ...
I want to keep in touch.
Katherine Smith Matheny

October 14

Go out and Climb a Mountain

Have you ever watched a sunrise
From a lofty mountaintop
And you felt so close to Heaven
You thought your heart would stop?
Have you sat and watched an eagle
Circle high above her nest
In a moment pure and simple
When you knew that you were blessed?
Have you stood atop the world
In the twilight's purple glow
And sent a prayer to Heaven
For people you don't know?

October 15 *

Now I Lay Me Down to Sleep

I remember so well this prayer I said
Each night as my mother tucked me in bed,
And today this same prayer is still the best way
To "sign off with God" at the end of the day.
And to ask Him your soul to ever keep
As you wearily close tired eyes to sleep
Feeling content that the Father above
Will hold you secure in His great arms of love ...
And having His promise that ere you wake
His angels will reach down your sweet soul to take

Is perfect assurance that awake or asleep
God is always right there to tenderly keep.
All His children are safe in His care
For God's here and He's there and He's everywhere ...
So, into His hands each night as I sleep
I commit my soul for the dear Lord to keep
Knowing that if my soul should take flight
It will soar to "the land where there is no night."

October 16 **

I Take His hand

Life, with all its ups and downs,
Can very disconcerting be;
But take the Savior's loving hand,
And He will care for thee.
When darkened cloudlets loom above,
Just think of Jesus and His love;
Then darkness seems to fall away
And ushers in a brighter day.
Dear Jesus, Lover of all life,
Oh, help me bear all stress and strife;
For when life fails to heed my plans,
I simply take Thine outstretched hand!
Sancie Earman King

October 17

The Meaning of Suffering

No one can be completely free of pain, says Canon R. C. Stephens, but our suffering can bring us closer to Christ

However much we resent pain, no one can be completely free from it; it comes to us all at some time or other, either physically, mentally or spiritually. It is a part of life – we enter the world through it and many leave it in the same manner. However unpleasant it is, let us not forget that without it, it would be impossible to know if anything was wrong with our bodies; it is an early warning system. Pain hurts, so we do our best to avoid it, and most households have their favorite brand of pain-killer. Suffering can have a devastating effect on us; if it is very severe, we find it difficult to think or concentrate. Everything tends to revolve around our condition, and we indulge in self-pity and selfishness.

Jesus took away the sufferings of others. He cured lepers of their disease. He raised the widow's son to life at Nain (*Luke 7:15*) and relieved her of great anguish. And out His compassion, there has grown medical science and research.

Jesus' attitude to His own physical suffering was quite different. He accepted the fact that He had come to suffer for the world's salvation and shocked His disciples when he spoke of His inevitable death. At His crucifixion He refused the drugged wine which would have lessened His pain (*Matthew 27:34*), not in any heroic or stoical way; but that He might taste pain and death to the full for everyone (*Hebrews 2:9*). The appalling pain He endured did not turn Him from caring for those around Him (*Luke 23:34*), He comforted a dying man and He looked after His beloved mother. What an example He gives us!

We are sometimes tempted to ask, "Why should I suffer?", but as followers of Christ that is a question we have to learn not to ask, for the New Testament shows that suffering will be the lot of the Christian who teaches that in some mysterious way we are then in fellowship with Christ (*Philippians 3:10*) and share in His sufferings (1 Peter 4:13), and He gives us strength to endure.

October 18

A Prayer for Healing

Lord, You invite all who are burdened to come to You.
Allow Your healing hand to heal me.
Touch my soul with Your compassion for others.
Touch my heart with Your courage and infinite love for all.
Touch my mind with Your wisdom,
that my mouth may always proclaim Your praise.
Teach me to reach out to You in my need,
and help me to lead others to You by my example.
Most loving Heart of Jesus, bring me health in
body and spirit that I may serve You with all my strength.
Touch gently this life which You have created,
Now and forevermore. Amen

October 19

Before it is Too Late

If you have a tender message
Or a loving word to say
Do not wait until you forget it,
But whisper it today;
The tender word unspoken,
The letter never sent,
The long forgotten messages,
The wealth of love unspent –
For these some hearts are breaking,
For these some loved ones wait;
So, show that you care for them
Before it is too late.
Frank Herbert Sweet

October 20 *

Troubled Waters

When I tread on troubled waters
And my faith begins to wane,
With His help I'll rise above it,
He is with me, praise His name.
He will hold my hand in trouble,
He will weep with me in sorrow
And He'll promise that a brighter day
Is in store for me tomorrow.
There is no one I can go to

For the comfort He can give,
He will always be there with me
Till on earth I no more live.
Then He'll gently lift me upwards
Onto His Father's throne,
Where my pain and heartaches are behind me
In my eternal home.
Albert N. Theel

October 21 *

Quiet Things

Lord, grant me the quiet things of life
That bring a sense of peace, not strife;
A tranquil hill of velvet green,
A robin's song, a pastoral scene.
The hush that comes at break of day
Before the rush of work and play;
The quiet patter of the rain
That dances on my windowpane.
The afterglow of sunset sky.
A mother's tender lullaby;
A time of prayer, a loved one's smile,
Contentment from a day worthwhile.
Amid life's noise and hurried pace,
Help us find time for calming grace
Of quiet things that bring release
And give to us an inner peace.
Beverly J. Anderson

October 22

The Heart of the Matter

Loving our neighbor sounds simple, says Canon R. C. Stephens,
but if we follow this principle closely we will see how important it
is and what contentment it brings

When we study the life of Jesus, we find that contrary to
what we might imagine, He seldom answered people's questions directly – at first it probably seemed that He evaded the
point, but far from taking evasive action, He always went to
the heart of the matter. When a man approached Him with the
request, "Speak to my brother, that he divide the inheritance
with me," Jesus refused and answered, "Take heed, and beware
of covetousness" (*Luke 12:13-15*). In other words, if the man
had observed the tenth commandment, there would have been
no need for anyone to intervene, for the problem would not
have arisen. What we do depends on the kind of person we
are – good actions are the fruits of a good life and vice versa.
"Make the tree good, and his fruit good ... for the tree is known
by his fruit" (Matthew 12:33). This is often what we refuse to
do. We are content to live with our unpleasant habits – being
rude to other people, getting angry at them, not being strictly
truthful and other things which spoil our lives but we are un-
willing to face the root of the problem – our inability to love
our neighbor. The way to better our lives is not to deal with
our faults one by one, but by making sure that the principles
by which we live are right and then most of our difficulties will
disappear.

October 23

Let Not Your Heart be Troubled

Let not your heart be troubled,
Give your worries and cares to Me.
I am your heavenly Father
Who suffered and died for thee.
There are times throughout your earthly life
When you are filled with doubts and fear.
Always come to Me in prayer
And know that I am near.
The love I have for you, dear child,
Can never be brought or measured.
It's a gift I freely give to you.
It is My most precious treasure.
When sorrow and pain come your way
And life seems to be unfair,
Let not your heart be troubled ...
Just come to Me in prayer.
Shirley Hile Powell

October 24

My Prayer of Acceptance

Dear Lord Jesus,
I do believe You are the Son of God.
Thank you for giving Your life in my place on the cross.
At this moment I choose to go Your way rather than my own.
I place my complete faith in You and invite You
To come in and take control of my life.
Thank You for coming and for the best
Christmas gift ever – Your gift of Eternal Life.
Help me to be faithful in reading Your Word, the Bible,
And praying each day so that others will see Jesus Christ in me.
I pray in Your name. Amen.

October 25

God's Amazing Gift to You

God wants you to be eternally related to Him.
He wants you in His family.
God wants to give you a new life
That begins here and now and goes on forever.
This amazing gift becomes yours when you:
... admit to God that you are a sinner,
but that you want to go His way from now on.
... accept the forgiveness and unconditional love
He offers you through Jesus Christ, and
... invite Jesus Christ to come in and
Take up residence in your life.

October 26 **

God Kept On Giving!

When Jesus Christ rose from the grave and
went back to Heaven to be with His Heavenly Father,
God gave His Holy Spirit
to live with man forever.
God's Holy Spirit will guide us so
We make the right choices;
He will comfort us when we are hurt;
He will guide us into All Truth!
The Holy Spirit gives us the power to
overcome every circumstance of life as He lives in us.
In Heaven, Jesus Christ is preparing a place for each one
who gives Him His rightful place in our lives.

October 27

God's Beautiful World

*We should work to increase beauty in our daily lives, says
Canon R. C. Stephens*

As this is God's world, we hold it in our trust for Him, and
it is therefore important how we treat it. If we hoard our possessions and keep them for ourselves, we become mean; if we
waste them, we become selfish; if we misuse them and bring
suffering to others, we are callous. Material things supply the
needs of people and take the drudgery and danger out of work,
but that is not all. Usefulness is not the only way of judging the
right use of earth's possessions.

The Psalmist wrote of "bread which strengtheneth man's heart" (*Psalm 104:15*), not his body, but his heart – his inner self. When dwellings are ugly or badly planned, the occupants suffer from depression; machinery may be functional yet soul-destroying; environment affects people mentally and spiritually. Plato, the Athenian philosopher (*427-347 B.C.*), said that to allow people to live in ugly surroundings was like keeping cattle in a foul pasture.

It may cost more to make things of good and pleasing design, but beauty is not an extra to life, it is part of God's plan. He made the world not only interesting and fascinating but also beautiful with flowers, trees, animals and birds, and we can be thankful for the increased interest in conservation, for if beauty disappears, the whole of life is impoverished. Jesus knew the importance of God's creation and told His disciples to "Consider the ravens: for they neither reap nor sow; ... consider the lilies ... they toil not, they spin not" (*Luke 12: 24, 27*).

We may feel that we cannot add to the beauty of the world, yet when the tabernacle was to be made, God involved the talents of ordinary men and women to beautify the sanctuary (*Exodus 35: 22-26*). In the same way He can use us to increase beauty in our daily lives; in our gardens, our homes, in music and handicrafts, and in many other ways.

October 28

Money

Money will buy a bed, but not sleep;
Books, but not knowledge;
Food, but not appetite;

Finery, but not beauty;
Amusement, but not happiness;
Religion, but not salvation;
You can buy a passport to anywhere except Heaven.

October 29

My Heart's Prayer

In the dawning of this new year,
It brings such joy within
To see where you have brought me, Lord –
From places where I've been.
You always walk beside me, Lord.
You dry my every tear.
You light the path before me.
You chase away my fears.
Each day is such a precious gift.
Oh, may I live each day
So full of joy and purpose,
As You guide me on life's way.
Mary Ann Jameson

October 30

My Heart's Prayer

Lord, I give you my fears,
please give me your strength.

October 31

Heavenly Father,
May we realize that your will
can never take us,
where grace cannot cover us.
Amen

November

Death is but a bend in the road,
not the end of the road.

November 1

Each Day Brings a Chance to Do Better

How often we wish for another chance
to make a fresh beginning,
A chance to blot out our mistakes
and change failure into winning –
And it does not take a special time
to make a brand-new start,
It only takes the deep desire
to try with all our heart
To live a little better
and to always be forgiving
And to add a little "sunshine"
to the world in which we're living –
So never give up in despair
and think that you are through,
For there's always a tomorrow
And a chance to start anew.

November 2

River of Life

We on the River of Life sail by,
Bound for the mystic Sea.
Many will stray from the Charted Way,
Missing the best to be.
Others will crash on the rocky shoals,
Stranded in pain and woe,

But there are some who continue on,
Close to the Lord they go.
He is the Pilot who marks the course
Right to the Port-of-Call.
He is the Leader at every turn
Ready to help us all.
Only the Savior can safely guide
Us to that shining sea ...
And He will rescue each soul who cries,
"Jesus, I trust in Thee."

November 3

Heavenly Treasure

Canon R. C. Stephens explains to us the joy to be found in generosity with possessions, time and money

Many people claim that they dislike shopping, but nevertheless, will happily buy a new coat or pair of shoes; and men who hate buying clothes will eagerly buy things for their garden or hobby. Our generation collects more articles than any previous age and one might think that such possessions would bring satisfaction, but those people with many often seem to be very unhappy and discontented.

Jesus warned us that possessions only increase worry by attracting thieves to break in and steal (*Matthew 6:19*). A church had a number of precious things and one by one they disappeared until none were left. "I'm sorry they've gone," said the vicar, "but in a way it's a relief for now I can open the church without worrying."

When Jesus said, "Lay up for yourselves treasures in heaven," where nothing could attack them, He was advocating a completely different principle of living – giving, not gathering. People who want these heavenly treasures must first give themselves to the Lord (*2 Corinthians 8:5*), and then make giving a principle of living – giving their money, time and service for others, and it is remarkable the joy such people discover, "the joy which no man taketh from you" (*John 16:22*).

The Sea of Galilee is sparkling and alive because it continually pours its waters into the Jordan; while the Dead Sea is unhealthy and never gives its waters away, hoarding all that comes to it.

Jesus was the Father's gift to the world, "God so loved the world that He gave his only begotten Son," and Jesus gave His life for us all.

The Glory of Life is to love, not to be loved, to give, not to get, to serve, not to be served;

This is to know the Glory of Life."

November 4

An Old English Prayer

Give us, Lord, a bit o' sun,
a bit of work and a bit of fun;
Give us in all the struggle and sputter
our daily bread and a bit o' butter;
Give us health our keep to make,
An' a bit to spare for others sake;
Give us, too, a bit of song,
And a tale and a book to help us along.

Give us, Lord,
A chance to be, our goodly best,
brave, wise and free,
Our goodly best for ourselves, and others
Till all men learn to live as brothers

November 5

Death is but a bend in the road,
not the end of the road.
(This was the last passage I read to my mother
less than two weeks before her death in 2010.
She told me she used to write it on sympathy cards– *Billy*)

November 6

Beyond Reason

There are still many things in life which defy explanation, comments Canon R. C. Stephens

We live in an enquiring age – we want to know why things happen. We are not rational beings and God gave us enquiring minds which we feel give us the right to know about everything but there are certain things which defy explanation. Many do not like to think that some things are spontaneous and mistrust what cannot be explained.

We go through life for years meeting and greeting others and then suddenly one person is singled out from the rest and we realize that he or she is rather special. We are swept along in our friendship and love quite certain that here is someone unique. We do not analyze our feelings, indeed it is doubtful if we could but we know that here is one who is a friend or partner for life. We can give no reasons – we just know.

It is much the same with the appreciation of beauty. We cannot explain why a picture is beautiful – to us it just is and no more can be said. We do not draw up a balance sheet for and against it to prove its loveliness. We may point out certain features which attract us but these are not reasons.

When Jesus began His work He invited men to be with Him (*John 1: 38-48*) and when they were acquainted He called them to leave their homes and occupations and throw in their lot with Him – there was no argument or discussion. It may have seemed madness to them and against their better judgement, yet they obeyed because they were drawn irresistibly to Him by His magnetic personality. When they deserted Him, common sense told them that they had placed themselves beyond His reach, but His forgiving love would not let them go. The whole story of Jesus and His apostles is irrational and illogical according to the world's standards and we are grateful that it is, for following Him does not depend on reason or understanding.

Every Christian's relationship with Christ is irrational – why should He love us? – but He does and we shall never know what He finds attractive in us.

November 7 * *

> May God's joy, which the world cannot give and
> which the world cannot take away,
> be yours today and in all life's tomorrows.

#

Optimism is positive thinking lighted up.
Norman Vincent Peale

November 8

Precious Father,
Help me to learn to leave the "whys" of life to you
so I can live each day to the fullest.
In Jesus name, Amen.

###

It takes both rain and sunshine to make a rainbow.

November 9

The Power of Jesus' Touch

As discarded objects can be rescued and restored, so Jesus can give new value to apparently worthless lives, according to Canon R.C Stephens

In an age when so many things are used once and then thrown away, it is a problem to know what should be preserved. Often things that have escaped the dustbin have a habit of turning up years later as collector's pieces. Some things acquire added value through association with famous people. A few years ago I was given two brass candlesticks by a friend who had worked for the Browning household, and she assured me they had once belonged to Robert Browning, the poet. No longer are they just candlesticks; to me they are special.

When some of Christ's enemies planned to catch Him out, they asked: "Is it lawful to give tribute to Caesar or not?" and He replied, "Bring Me a penny" (*Mark 12:13-17*). T. R. Glover (*1869-1943*), formerly a don at Cambridge, was once shown a collection of Roman coins and was told that a "penny" issued at the time of Tiberius Caesar (*AD 14-37*) always commanded a higher price because Jesus might possibly have held it in His hand. We may smile that such an improbability should affect the value of a coin, but the incident is a parable.

There are numerous references in the gospels to Jesus touching people, and in every instance, they have changed for the better. When He gave sight to the blind, they no longer had to be led by the hand; when He laid His hands on the sick, they returned to normal living; and what a difference he made to Zaccheus, the publican, when he put His touch upon his life! (*Luke 19:2-10*).

And the good news today is that His "touch has still its ancient power." As people find rubbish, dirty and broken, which they clean and mend to become collectors' items, so Jesus collects the human debris of lives, apparently worthless, and recreates them to be of inestimable worth. He doesn't want dead museum pieces, but living souls who will influence others for Him by "the words they speak, the prayers they breathe and the life they live."

November 10

The Wheat and the Chaff

If we learn to discard the non-essentials of life, says Canon R. C. Stephens, we may devote more time to serving God and our fellow human beings

An aunt of mine, anxious not to be over-burdened with luggage when going away, always went through the clothes she was taking and asked, "Is your journey really necessary?" In this way she eliminated many articles which otherwise she would have had to carry with her.

Again and again, we are faced with the problem of which things and actions are necessary and which are not, if we are to remain faithful to the primary reason for being alive, namely, to do God's will.

Jesus came to do the Father's will (*John 6:38*), and the Gospels illustrate his clear mind. They show that he never allowed Himself to be side-tracked by non-essentials, nor did He concern Himself with the trivial. He needed the four basic requirements of food, clothing, shelter and security as much as anyone, but He could never take them for granted.

He accepted what food was given to Him: He had only the clothes he stood up in; often He must have slept under the stars; and for security, He had none. His 'meat' was to do the will of Him that sent Him (*John 4:34*), so He was ready to do without such 'necessities'. Christ not only conquered sin, He overcame all the less important and the irrelevant things of life.

Having had to move houses many times, I know only too well how easy it is to accumulate unnecessary things because the dustbin is not used properly. A Christian must have a dustbin, as it were, not only for what is wrong, but also for rubbish and the things which don't matter much. Life is full and interesting, and we must discriminate between the essential and the non-essential, otherwise we soon get bogged down with incidentals and there will be little time or opportunity for serving Christ and others.

November 11

The Law and the Spirit

We need to add Christ's spirit to the letter of the law to improve the quality of life, says Canon R. C. Stephens

It is extraordinary that the tremendous amount of the law in the Old Testament can be summed up in two short commandments: Thou shalt love the Lord thy god, and thy neighbor as thyself. Furthermore, the two depend on each other, for the test of my love for God is to be found in answer to the question, "Do I love my neighbor?"

The second summarized the detailed instructions dealing with all matters, from seeing that the poor shared in the harvest to the requirement of a parapet when building a house, as a safety measure. All this helped to bring about a more civilized life for everybody, but it didn't make the people kinder to each other or more compassionate. It was possible to obey the law and yet omit love itself.

In New Testament times the people kept to the letter of the law and Jesus warned them, "unless you show yourselves far better men than the Pharisees and the doctors ... you can never enter the kingdom of Heaven" (*Matthew 5:20*). He came to fulfill the law by introducing a new spirit.

When a lawyer asked, "Who is my neighbor?" Jesus told a story about a Samaritan, an outsider, who not only helped but brought compassion to an injured traveler, even paying the bill at an inn until he had fully recovered, while a priest and a Levite had left the man to die. It was the spirit of love and kindness that mattered so much to Jesus that He actually gave a new commandment – "That ye love one another" (*John 13:34*).

Today the law is far more comprehensive in its support of the afflicted and the poor, which is in keeping with the second commandment, but we also need Christ's spirit to bring what legislation never can – love. Christian people must show this love, not only to the unfortunate but to those who are particularly unpleasant as well, if the world is to become a happier and more peaceful place to live in.

November 12

God's Gift of Love

God blesses me in so many ways
I can never repay,
And I thank Him with all my heart
Each morn and close of day.
I never can be worthy
Of all the gifts of love,
That He bestows upon me
From His great realm above.
Despite all the sins that I possess
And wrong that I may do,
He blesses and forgives me
Day after day anew.

> Though oft I fall I fail Him
> And sinner that I may be,
> He never fails to show His love
> And blessings unto me.
> *Harold F. Mohn*

November 13

> An open mind opens the opportunity
> of dropping a worthwhile thought into it.

#

> A soft answer turneth away wrath.

November 14

> Lord, I believe that all things are possible
> With you in my life.
> I surrender the "impossible" to you today.

November 15

The Chosen Ones

There is a place in God's pattern for even the most ordinary of us, explains Canon R. C. Stephens

It is strange that our Lord chose the men He did to be His apostles, for none of them was exceptional. In fact, they were very ordinary – fishermen, a tax collector, an agitator and so on, so that it is tempting to ask, "Were these the best that He could find?"

In the list of apostles' names in the Gospels, some are never heard of again. He must have known what they were like before calling them, which makes His choice of them even more remarkable. Even the conviction that Jesus was "the Christ, the Son of the living God (*Matthew 16:16*) made no difference in their attitude toward Him. They contradicted Him and, although lacking faith themselves, did not hesitate to stop another who was affecting cures, because he was not sure of them (*Luke 9:49*).

They argued over the leadership, presumably anticipating their Master's death and after spending three years in His company, He could no more rely on them than at the beginning of His ministry – one betrayed, one denied Him, and all deserted Him.

It is in their ordinariness that we find a clue as to why they were chosen. If Christ had chosen brilliant organizers, sophisticated men with clever minds, those with exceptional gifts, it would have been so much more difficult for others to follow. Someone has said, "God must love ordinary people very much because He made so many of them." Christ chose people like ourselves, people with our weaknesses, without special qualities and who were frail like us.

When I realize this, I am glad that Christ chose as He did because if He could choose commonplace men for such important work, then there is hope for us, too. In the apostles' earthly frailties I see my own – my pride, my lack of faith, my prejudices and self-seeking.

But, I cannot shelter under the knowledge that I am no worse, because those apostles we read about did not stay ordinary but, through the Holy Spirit, became extraordinary. And if God could change them into saints, He could change us, too, into more loving people – if we would only let Him.

November 16

Faith in a Changing World

In spite of the continual changes which occur in life, God remains always the same, Canon R. C. Stephens reminds us

The world is, as it has always been, constantly changing. But during the past fifty years, the changes have been more and numerous and more rapid than in previous centuries. This is particularly noticeable in our standard of living and in technical advancement. Much of what has happened has brought comfort and help to many people, which was long overdue, as for example, advances in medical care, or women receiving equal pay for doing the same work as men.

In the moral and spiritual sphere, however, we find it difficult to assimilate change. This is nothing new, for many in the first century A.D. found the teaching of Jesus destructive in spite of His saying, "Think not that I am come to destroy the law, or the prophets: I am not come to destroy, but to fulfill (*Matthew 5:17*).

Perhaps this may have been Nicodemus' concern when he visited Jesus secretly, for to him the law had been given by God and the religious leaders had worked out its applications. He must have found disturbing reports of Jesus's preachings that to be angry with another without cause was almost as serious as murder, and that charitable works did not break the Sabbath but that the impure thought broke the seventh commandment. Such teaching must have represented a radical change to him.

Today Christians everywhere are finding great changes taking place – with the new translations of the Bible, favorite texts do not seem to ring with the same certainty; often our worship seems different; cherished beliefs about personal relationships are discarded. Many people find this very upsetting and the foundations of their faith are shaken. But, God is the same, He has not changed – a fact of which the prophet Malachi reminds us, "I am the Lord, I change not." (*Malachi 3:6*). It is upon God that we have to build our lives amidst all the change that continuously goes on around us.

November 17

Kindness is like a boomerang.
It always returns.

#

O God, my Maker, from whom I hold my life in trust,
give me this day the grace I may need to stand for thee openly,
to serve thee faithfully and follow thee fearlessly.

November 18

Time and again, Jesus demonstrated
Just how breath-taking the power of prayer can be.

#

Dear God, I pray for the strength to endure
the stoplights in life.
Please help me to turn to You for direction,
teaching, and hope, during these times.

November 19

The Power of Prayer

Canon R. C. Stephens reminds us that prayer works no matter what the circumstances

Many of us often feel that there are certain things which we can probably accomplish – and prayer could be useful in helping us to do so – but we don't believe that prayer could assist us to carry out something which seems hopelessly beyond our capabilities.

We tend to limit the power of prayer to a possibly beneficial "extra", or bonus not to be expected but pleasant if it is received. Actually, there is no limit to the scope and range of the transformation prayer can bring.

Jesus said that the things which are impossible with men are possible with God (*Mark 10:27*). His firm belief in the power of prayer for every kind of situation is quite breath-taking. He declared that faith could move mountains, and he wanted us to have the same massive confidence in prayer and the Father's love and care as he had. Part of his task was to reveal the nature of God and hold on to his faith through all the suffering and misunderstanding which it was necessary for him to endure, right up to the Cross.

Bishop Phillip Brooks once urged us, "Do not pray for tasks equal to your powers. Pray for powers equal to your tasks." In his temptations in the wilderness and later in the garden of Gethsemane, Jesus prayed that He might be given power equal to that task. God's answer was the Resurrection and the birth of the Christian Church.

Someone once said that we don't usually ask God for *big* enough things. If our God is too small, then our prayers will often be too small as well. Prayer, like life itself, is a venture in which we really have to launch into the deep.

November 20

Old Irish Blessing

May the road rise up to meet you.
May the wind be always at your back.
May the sunshine warm your face
And rains fall soft upon your fields.
And until we meet again,
May God hold you in the hollow of His hand.

November 21

My Prayers are with You

I take your name to God in prayer
More often than you'd guess.
I ask Him to watch over you,
Protect, care for and bless.
I pray He'll keep you happy,
And in His goodness give
The gifts of hope and faith and love
That make life sweet to live.

Jan Gilbert

November 22

Looking for Good

Our view of others can reflect our own characters, suggests David M. Owen

It is said that Aesop, the brilliant writer of fables, was sitting beside the road one day when a stranger walked up and asked the way to Athens, and also what the people were like there. Aesop replied, "Certainly, but first I must ask where you come from and how you find the people there."

"I come from Argos," said the man, "and the people of Argos are bad characters, dishonest, immoral and unfriendly."

"I am sorry to tell you," said Aesop, "that you will find the Athenians just the same." With that he showed him on his way.

Presently, another man came up to him with the same request, and Aesop replied as he had with the first. "I come from

Argos," said the man. "and the people of Argos are good people, so honest, helpful and friendly."

"I am delighted to tell you," said Aesop, "that you will find the people of Athens just the same."

I have just returned to England from Dallas, Texas. The city, like any other city, had its badness, and a fair share of problems. But I have found the people of Dallas, in shops, in offices, banks and elsewhere – not least in the churches – to be extremely kind and helpful.

For isn't it true that we often find just what we are looking for, whether it is good or bad, and that what we discover is but a reflection of our own character and personality?

Jesus saw goodness where others saw wrong, beauty where others saw ugliness. Zaccheus and Levi were tax collectors whom others despised, but Jesus looked for the goodness in them – and found it.

How easy it can be for us to become critical of people and places. We look for faults and, of course, we find them. So, too, do others find them in us. Wouldn't it be a pleasant change to reverse our outlook and seek goodness?

Jesus gave us a commandment: "Love one another, as I have loved you" (*John 15:12*): I think we should try to follow it.

November 23

Blessings of Forgetfulness

There are times when only by forgetting the past can we go on living meaningful lives, Rev. David M. Owen tells us.

Forgetfulness can land us in all sorts of trouble – a forgotten appointment or anniversary – so it is useful to be blessed with a good memory. But there is a sense in which we all need to cultivate the spirit of forgetfulness.

Much of the trouble in our world is caused not by things forgotten which should have been remembered, but by things remembered which should have been forgotten.

Henri Bergson, the French philosopher, said, "It is a function of the brain to enable us not to remember, but to forget." What if the stunning blows we receive in life should never lose their initial sting? Wouldn't we find life unbearable? Only by forgetting are we able to go on living purposeful lives.

A moving story comes out of World War II. In April 1942, Jacob De Shazer, along with other airmen, bombed Japan. Later their fuel ran out and they were forced to land in China. Captured by Japanese, they were imprisoned, starved and tortured. They were filled with hatred and revenge. Then one day a Japanese Christian handed them a Bible. They read it, for it was their only reading matter in solitary confinement. Jacob De Shazer read the words of Jesus: "This is my commandment, that ye love one another, as I have loved you" (*John 15:12*). Then he describes how the bitterness went from him and how he felt that this text meant something special for him: " I knew I had to come back to Japan when the war was over and bring the gospel of Christ with me."

In 1945, he was released, went through missionary training college and in 1948 went with his wife to Japan, this time armed with the Bible. At one meeting he recognized hatred in the eyes of a Japanese girl, and he knew the time had come to confess how Christ had turned his hate into love and why he had come to Japan. The Japanese girl was impressed enough to become a Christian herself, and then admitted that she had come to kill the American in revenge for her sweetheart, who had been killed by American bombs.

Many things are best forgotten in the forgiving love of Christ.

November 24

A Matter of Influence

When He created us, God established the principle of mutual dependence and influence, explains Canon R. C. Stephens

In creating us, God established the principle that "none of us liveth to himself" (*Romans 14:7*). In other words, we depend on each other and once we grab this, prayer, which is a problem to many, becomes easier to understand. For if we unknowingly effect the lives of others, how much more will we do so when we pray intentionally for their benefit.

We have all benefitted from those who have lived before us, and we in turn influence others by what we do and say. Often we do not know that this is happening, and are surprised to be told that people have been encouraged by our example.

In 1936, a man was found dead on the Thames embankment. His sole possession was a letter written to him in 1911 by W. R. Shepphard (later to become the Rev. Dick Sheppard), which he had carried in his pocket for twenty-five years, and it had no doubt been a comfort to the end.

Dick Sheppard could not possibly have anticipated the effect of his letter, yet most of us have cause to thank God for friends who have wittingly or unwittingly helped us.

It is when we realize what a bad effect our doings can have that we become aware of our responsibility to others. Our actions are like stones thrown into a pond and as, the ripples go out in ever increasing circles, so the consequences of our deeds are spread.

November 25

Lord God, who art even beyond
the uttermost reaches of space,
help us recognize Thee everywhere.
Father, who hast made us in Thine image,
Encourage us to approach Thee
In spirit and truth. Amen.

#

Lord, you showed us
your brokenness on the cross.
Help us to accept
Our own brokenness
And bring it to you for
Healing only You can give.
Amen

November 26

A Nun's Prayer

Lord, thou knowest better than I know myself that I am growing older and someday will be old. Keep me from the fatal habit of thinking I must say something on every subject and on every occasion. Release me from craving to straighten out everybody's affairs. Make me thoughtful not moody; helpful but not bossy. With my vast store of wisdom, it seems a pity not to use it all, but Thou knowest Lord that I want a few friends at the end.

Keep my mind from the recital of endless details; give me wings to get to the point. Seal my lips on my aches and pains.

They are increasing, and love of rehearsing them is becoming sweeter as the years go by. I dare not ask for grace enough to enjoy the tales of others' pains, but help me to endure them with patience.

I dare not ask for improved memory, but for a growing humility and a lessing cocksureedness when my memory seems to clash with the memories of others. Teach me the glorious lesson that occasionally I may be mistaken.

Keep me reasonably sweet; I do not want to be a Saint – some of them are so hard to live with – but a sour old person is one of the crowning works of the devil.

Give me the ability to see good things in unexpected places, and talents in unexpected people. And give me, O Lord, the grace to tell them so. Amen

November 27

Our Prayer of Thanks

We humbly bow before You, Lord
On this Thanksgiving Day,
To lift our prayers of gratitude
For all Your caring ways.
As You have blessed our harvest, Lord,
Let us remember, too,
That we should share with those in need
As You would have us do.
Around this festive board today
Are those we hold most dear,
And in our midst Your presence, Lord,
Seems so very near.
We're thankful for this land we love,
For sod and sky and tree,
For Pilgrims who braved unknown seas
That all may worship free.
We're thankful for each blessing, Lord,
You send along our way;
But may our greater "thanks" be shown
In serving You each day.
Kay Hoffman

November 28

The Great Provider

God provides with His largess
For all life here below,
Our daily food and provender
To utilize and stow.
From tiny seedlings in the ground
Planted with such care,
He sends the rain and sunshine down
To help them ripen there.
When the days of Autumn come
And the crop is gathered in,
Bin and silo have their fill
Of plenty once again.
For every gift from God above,
May I always thankful be,
Expressing gratitude and love
For His generosity.
Elsie Natalie Brady

November 29

Prayer of Thanksgiving

For letting us live
in the beam of Thy love,
For manifold blessings
of Thine from above
Dear Lord, we thank Thee.

For beauties of nature
this world so fair
For glories of God
which abound everywhere
Dear Lord, we thank Thee
For tasks accomplished –
pleasures earned
For ambitions high,
and lessons learned;
For kindness and humility,
For measure of tranquility;
For peace of fireside and home –
Safe keeping when we need to roam;
For children and joys we find
in rearing them; for peace of mind;
For all things good that come from Thee
Dear Lord, we thank Thee.

Pearl E. Auer

November 30

Thanksgiving Grace

We bow our heads dear Lord, to You,
For all the special things You do,
For all the brethren everywhere
We offer You this humble prayer.
Oh mighty Lord who art above
Bestow on us Thy gracious love,
Please bless us as we sit to dine
To break some bread and sip of wine.

For all these foods You do provide
Your presence cannot be denied,
We bow our heads in silent prayer
To have You know we really care.
We thank Thee Lord for all Thy good
You offer to all brotherhood,
And especially for this gathering,
We thank Thee Lord for everything.
Joseph Ferrara

December

Life is hard by the yard,
But it's a cinch by the inch.

December 1

Oh Father,
May the holy star
grow every year, more bright,
and send its glorious beam afar
to fill the world with light.
William Cullen Bryant

Advent

"Advent" from the Latin word *advenire*, means "the coming." When we come to the four Sundays in Advent, we are participating in spiritual preparation to celebrate the "coming" birth of Christ, the incarnation, God with us in the flesh to redeem our lives. Basically, Advent is a time to anticipate and prepare for Jesus' coming.

The Advent wreath and candles help us in our Advent preparation. The wreath is made of evergreen boughs, a sign of ever-new life, a sign of God's eternity: God is and always will be!

Three violet or purple candles are used – one for each of the first three Sundays in Advent – to remind us of Jesus' royalty and lordship. A rose-colored candle is used on the fourth Sunday to remind us of Mary, the mother of Jesus. A white candle is lighted on Christmas Day to symbolize the assurance of the abundant life we have in Christ. The candles symbolize Jesus' birth as the advent of Light, Peace and Life. (*If colored candles are not available, all white or all red candles may be used.*)

December 2

The Way to the Manger

Those who visited the stable on the first Christmas Day represented the whole of mankind, explains Canon R. C. Stephens

Why do we keep a special day each year in honor of Christ's birthday, and what made us put it at the cross-roads of history – between B.C. and A.D.? The answer is that God intervened in His world because He cared for His children so much and wanted them to know Him, and He arranged to come as a weak and helpless babe.

Just as a new-born child is welcomed in the home and brings hope and love to the family, so Jesus brought hope and love to the world. There was 'open house' at the stable, and the message of Christmas is that all are welcomed by God. "Emmanuel ... God with us" (*Matthew 1:23*).

Those who visited the manger at the first Christmas really represented us all. The simple-hearted shepherds on the hillside, ordinary people like us, were told that a Savior was born and would be found "lying in a manger". Without argument of ceremony, they rushed to see "this thing which is come to pass, which the Lord hath made known" (*Luke 2:15*). There are many today like them, who in simple faith accept Christ as the Son of God without question, and we are fortunate if we are among them.

But there are others with enquiring minds who long to believe but find too many questions unanswered. How like the Wise Men they are, who gazed at the heavens and studied their books to see what the star foretold before setting out. What doubts and problems must have arisen in their minds as they

271

journeyed! But because they sought the truth, they were led to the house and they fell down and worshipped.

Were they disappointed to find this king in such poor surroundings? As far as we know, these heathen philosophers did not believe in God, but their honest seeking brought them to Bethlehem. All who sincerely search for truth will eventually find Jesus, Who is the truth, to be the way and the life as well (*John 14:6*).

December 3

Loving Father, help us remember the birth of Jesus that we may share in the song of the angels, the gladness of the shepherds, and the worship of the wise men.

Close the door of hate and open the door of love all over the world.

Let kindness come with every gift and good desires with every greeting.

Deliver us from evil by the blessing which Christ brings, and teach us to be merry with clear hearts.

May the Christmas morning make us happy to be thy children, and the Christmas evening bring us to our beds with grateful thoughts, forgiving and forgiven, for Jesus sake. Amen

Robert Louis Stevenson

December 4

One Life

He was born in a stable in an obscure village,
From there he traveled less than 200 miles.
He never won an election.
He never went to college.
He never owned a home.
He never had a lot of money.
He became a nomadic preacher.
Popular opinion turned against Him.
He was betrayed by a close friend
And His other friends ran away.
He was unjustly condemned to death
Crucified on a cross among common thieves
On a hill overlooking the town dump.
And when dead, laid in a borrowed grave.
Nineteen centuries have come and gone.
Empires have risen and fallen.
Mighty armies have marched
And powerful rulers have reigned.
Yet no one has affected men as much as He.
He is the central figure of the human race.
He is the Messiah, the Son of God,
JESUS CHRIST

"He is the image of the unseen God.
And the first born of all creation.
For in Him were created all things,
In heaven and on earth" (*Colossians 1:15, 16*)
Kristone

December 5

The Greatest Gift

Canon R. C. Stephens reminds us of the simple message of Christmas

Over the Christmas period we will probably enjoy hearing again the simple story of Christ's birth at Bethlehem, a story which no matter how often we hear it still seems fresh and new. Often, in fact, to the busy housewife coping with extra shopping and preparation, it suddenly brings back the heart of Christmas, and an oasis of peace in what has become a very commercial time.

"He came down to earth from Heaven, Who is God and Lord of all." We do need to remind ourselves constantly in the hurly-burly of the season that Christmas is Christ's birthday. We give each other presents which is really the wrong way round; we should be giving to Him for it is His day. But, what can we give? Fortunately He has Himself told us what we can do when He said, "For I was hungry, and ye gave me meat: I was thirsty, and ye gave me drink: I was a stranger, and ye took me in: I was naked, and ye clothed me: I was sick, and ye visited me: I was in prison, and ye came unto me ... In as much as ye have done it unto one of the least of these my brethren, ye have done it unto me." (*Matthew 25:35-41*)

Sadly, we do not have to look far to discover the "least of His brethren" for the world is full of them – starving, homeless, orphaned, unhappy, unwanted, lonely handicapped – the list is endless, and the ways we can give Him a present on His birthday are numerous.

December 6

Christmas in the Heart

It is Christmas in the mansion
Yule log fires and silken frocks;
It is Christmas in the cottage,
Mothers filling little socks.
It is Christmas on the highway,
In the thronging, busy mart;
But the dearest truest Christmas
Is the Christmas in the heart.

December 7

The Priceless Gift of Christmas

The priceless gift of Christmas
is meant just for the heart
and we receive it only
when we become a part
of the kingdom and the glory
which is ours to freely take.
For God sent the Holy Christ Child

at Christmas for our sake,
so man might come to know Him
and feel His presence near
and see the many miracles
And this Priceless Gift of Christmas
is within the reach of all,
the rich, the poor, the young and old,
the greatest and the small.
So take His Priceless Gift of Love,
reach out and you receive,
and the only payment that God asks
is just that you believe.
Helen Steiner Rice

December 8

A Touch of Christmas

Keep a touch of Christmas
Tucked within your heart;
Keep a touch, but share a touch
With those both near and far.
For Christmas speaks of giving
To each and every one;
Did God not give at Christmas
His own beloved Son?
Keep a touch of Christmas
Tucked within your heart;
Let its sacred meaning
Ne'er from you depart.
Keep a touch, but share a touch

With those along life's way,
That each may come to realize
The truth of Christmas Day.
Loise Pinkerton Fritz

December 9

Christmas Morning

The bells ring clear as bugle note;
Sweet song is filling every throat;
'Tis welcome Christmas morning!
O, never yet was morn so fair;
Such silent music in the air;
'Tis Merry Christmas morning!
Dear day of all days in the year;
Dear day of song, good will and cheer;
"Tis golden Christmas Morning!
The hope, the faith, the love that is,
The peace the holy promises;
'Tis glorious Christmas morning!
Joaquin Miller

December 10

The Miracle of Christmas

The wonderment in a small child's eyes,
The ageless awe in the Christmas skies,
The nameless joy that fills the air,

The throngs that kneel in praise and prayer ...
These are the things that make us know
That men may come and men may go.
But none will ever find a way
To banish Christ from Christmas Day ...
For with each child there's born again
A *mystery* that baffles men.
Helen Steiner Rice

December 11

The Will to Succeed

We should not fear the Christian way of life is too hard for us – God will help us if we put our faith in Him, says Canon R. C. Stephens

How despondent we can feel when our plans do not come up to our expectations, and we have failed others and ourselves. Yet Kipling suggests in his poem, *If*, "that we should treat those two imposters (Triumph and Disaster) just the same". The successful businessman may find his home life has broken down, whereas the person who is a so-called failure may know a contentment envied by others. Nevertheless, we do set such great store by success that fear of failing can paralyze us into inactivity.

In the parable about the talents (these were coins of the time), the servant who was given one talent said to his master. "I was afraid, and went and hid thy talent in the earth: lo, there thou has that is thine" (*Matthew 25:25*). He was so anxious not to make a mistake that he did nothing. He only had to deposit the money with the exchangers, a simple transaction which did not require much skill, but fear prevented him. How many excellent schemes have never been started because someone could not bear the thought of failing!

There are those who will not venture upon the Christian way of life – not because they do not believe in it, they do, but because they are afraid, they would not reach the standard they consider necessary.

In truth, their fears are justified to the extent that none of us reach Christ's standard. But, we are not to ask ourselves, "Am I a good Christian?" for the judgement is His. It is obedience to Christ's call that really matters – *doing nothing* is failure. Our attempts may not be spectacular, but God has a knack of turning apparent failure into ultimate triumph.

When we celebrate the birth of Jesus Christ this Christmastide, let us remember how he came to inspire us all to use our talents to make the world a better place. And let us, with renewed courage, once again dedicate our lives to His service.

December 12

Of Fairest Joys – Christmas

The season marks a special time,
For soon be Christmas Day!
The fairest joys in all the world
Are spread in bright array:
The gifts beneath the Christmas tree,
The fireplace all aglow;
The candles lit upon the sill,
The stockings in a row.
The spicy smell of Christmas breads,

The pine that wafts the air –
There is a certain peace within
That makes the season rare.
The wind blows down the chimney flue,
The snow builds up amain –
And hearts are filled with Christmas cheer,
To have friends home again.
Roxie Lusk Smith

December 13

The Christ Child Comes to Us

Come in, come in, it's Christmas Day!
In glad harmony, let us now play
The song of love within our heart;
Tidings of great joy, we'll impart.
Come in, come in from out the cold,
And hear the most wonderous story told;
Of how one, glorious, star-filled night
The Christ Child came to give us light.
Come in, come in, my Jesus, sweet,
Into our hearts and there to greet
Love given in complete devotion,
Overflowing with tender emotion.
Come in Come in, Oh Holy Child!
Adorn our beings – make them mild.
Fill us with Your goodness and peace,
And songs of joy that never cease.
Dorothy Manziak

December 14

Christmas Is

Christmas is the sound of bells,
The laughter and the pageantry,
Soft falling snow and the fire light's glow
And the star on top of the tree.
Christmas is the sight of home,
The holly and the mistletoe,
Candlelight on the cold, crisp night
And "Merry Christmas" wherever you go.
Christmas is the smell of pine,
The turkey and the pumpkin pie,
Stockings hung and carols sung
And glittering star on high.
Christmas is the surge of hope,
Wee children's glee, tinseled Christmas tree ...
And love in your heart serene.
Nora M. Bozeman

December 15

The Scent of Pine

The scent of pine and candles,
The lights upon the tree,
The Merry Yuletide wishes
Spell Christmas time to me.
The mistletoe and holly,
The sound of laughter gay,

The gifts with fancy wrappings
Tell me it's Christmas Day.
Amidst the joy and merriment
I humbly kneel and pray,
And in my heart remember
That Christ was born this day.
Harold F. Mohn

December 16

The Miracle of Christmas

The miracle of Christmas,
With the hope and joy it brings,
Is evidenced throughout the world
As we welcome Christ the King.
With kind hearts overflowing
And gifts for old and young,
We're making cherished memories
While Christmas carols are sung.
May Baby Jesus, garbed in love,
Enfold you in His care,
And may goodwill and peace on earth
Be witnessed everywhere.
Catherine Janssen Irwin

December 17

Christmas

Christmas is the time of year
When families get together.
They come from near, and far away;
Regardless of the weather.
To share a special kind of joy,
That only Christmas brings:
Tasty foods, a lovely tree,
Exchanging gifts of special things.
It is a time of peace on earth;
Goodwill to everyone.
On this day our Lord was born.
God's own beloved Son.
Frances Culp Wolfe

December 18

Christmas Feeling

Oh, God, let me feel the joy of Christmas
As I have each coming year.
Let me feel its love and happiness
That will bring a tear.
Let me feel the Christ Child,
This miracle from above,
Let me wonder at this day
Filled with peace and love.
This, as every Christmastime,

I will be overcome with peace and joy,
When Christ, our Savior is come –
This blessed baby Boy.
James Joseph Huesgen

December 19

THE INCOMPARABLE CHRIST

He came from the bosom of the Father to the bosom of a woman. He put on humanity that we may have divinity. He became the Son of Man that we might become the sons of God.

He was born contrary to the laws of nature, lived in poverty, was reared in obscurity, and only once crossed the boundary of the land in childhood. He had no wealth or influence and had neither training nor education in the world's schools. His relatives were inconspicuous and uninfluential.

In infancy, He startled a king; in boyhood, He puzzled the learned doctors; in manhood, He ruled the course of nature. He walked upon the billows and hushed the sea to sleep. He healed the multitudes without medicine and made no charge for His services.

He never wrote a book, yet all the libraries in the country could not hold the books that have been written about Him. He never wrote a song, yet He has furnished the theme for more songs than all the songwriters together. He never founded a college, yet all the schools together cannot boast of as many students as He has. He never practiced medicine, and yet He healed more broken hearts than the doctors have healed broken bodies.

He is the Star of astronomy, the Rock of geology, the Lion and the Lamb of zoology, the Harmonizer of all discords, and the Healer of all diseases. Great men have come and gone, yet He lives on. Herod could not kill Him; Satan could not seduce Him; death could not destroy Him; the grave could not hold Him.

He was rich, yet for our sakes became poor. How poor? Ask Mary. Ask the wise men. He slept in another's manger; He cruised the lake in another's boat; He rode on another man's ass; He was buried in another man's tomb. He is the ever perfect One. He is altogether lovely.

December 20

A Cowboy's Christmas Prayer

I ain't much good at prayin', and you may not know me, Lord.
I ain't much seen in churches where they preach
Thy Holy Word.
But you may have observed me, out here on the lonely plains,
Alookin' after cattle, feeling thankful when it rains.
Admirin' Thy great handiwork, the miracle of grass,
Aware of Thy kind spirit in the way it comes to pass.
That hired men on horseback and the livestock that we tend
Can look up at the stars at night and know we have a Friend.
So here's ol' Christmas comin' on remindin' us again
Of Him whose coming brought good will into the
hearts of men.
A cowboy ain't no preacher, but if you'll hear my prayer,
I'll ask as good as we have got for all men everywhere.
Don't let no hearts be bitter, Lord, don't let no child be cold.

Make easy beds for them that's sick, and them that's
weak and old.
Let kindness bless the trail we ride, no matter what we're after,
And sorter keep us on Your side, in tears as well as laughter.
I'm just a sinful cowpoke, Lord, ain't got no business prayin'
But still I hope You'll ketch a word or two of what I'm asayin'
We speak of Merry Christmas, Lord, I reckon you'll agree
There ain't no Merry Christmas for nobody that isn't free.
So one more thing I'll ask you Lord: Just help us when you can
To save some seeds of freedom for the future sons of man.

December 21

Christmas

Christmas is a time for us
To renew our faith and love.
Herald angels sing their praises
To the Lord above.
Ringing bells are sounding
To proclaim His birth today.
In our hearts we feel His love,
And with us He will stay.
So, on this day as we celebrate,
May we feel His inner peace.
Together we will share a love
That will never cease.
May all the earth proclaim the Lord

And give glory to Him above
So the world will always know
The power of His love.
Sue Pagnanella

December 22

Talking With God

Prayer should be a conversation with a friend, says Canon R. C. Stephens, and we should not only talk to him, but listen as well

Prayer is the most important part of the Christian life. It is our lifeline, keeping us spiritually alive. However, many find difficulty in praying and some give up. Yet nowhere in the New Testament are difficulties mentioned. It is assumed that Christians pray and apparently find it easy and uncomplicated to do so. Why then do so many find problems today? I believe it is because many have wrong ideas about prayer.

The principle of prayer is very simple – it is a conversation with a friend. Many think prayer is chiefly concerned with making requests of God. Requests have their place in the conversation; as St. Paul said, "let your requests be made known to God" (*Philippians 4:6*). But a friendship which only consists in asking will never grow or develop. Most of us have experienced the person who takes over the conversation so that others cannot get a word in; some prayers must seem like that to God. If our prayers are chiefly for our loved ones and ourselves, no wonder we find prayer dull.

When the disciples asked Jesus, "Lord, teach us to pray" (*Luke 11:1*), He gave them the Lord's Prayer as a pattern, a pattern which many largely ignore. It is worth noticing that in it there is only one request for material needs and two for our spiritual advancement, forgiveness and deliverance from evil. The emphasis in the "Our Father" is on God, His Glory, His Kingdom, and His will, and by this Christ extended the scope of prayer enormously. Yet these are frequently omitted by those who pray. St. Paul said we should pray "for all men, for Kings and for all who are in authority" (*1 Timothy 21:1,2*), which means praying for God's Kingdom and that His will should be done.

Our friendship with an earthly friend depends chiefly on two things. First on meeting each other and secondly, on talking together. Our friendship with God is based on the same two things. Prayer gives us the opportunity of meeting with God at any moment, for He is always by our side. Prayer is chatting with Him on everything, provided we do not monopolize the conversation, but let Him have His say.

December 23

Jesus

There He lies in unseen glory
Just beginning His love story
Snuggled in a manger bed
Mary's little sleepyhead
King of kings without a throne
Born to rule our hearts alone
Clad in swaddle, yet divine
Come to claim your heart and mine
Margaret Peterson

December 24

An Ancient English Carol
A child is born in Bethlehem;
Rejoice, therefore Jerusalem.
Low in the manger lieth He,
Whose kingdom without end shall be.
All glory, Lord, to Thee be done,
Now seen in flesh, the Virgin's Son.

December 25

Harken! Harken!

Oh, hear the bells on Christmas morn,
They tell us that a King is born.
Behold a bright and gleaming star –
Oh, come and worship from afar.
See a Virgin Mother mild,
See a meek and holy child,
Oh, hear the bells on Christmas ring –
What joyous news to men they bring!
Oh, hear the bells on Christmas Day,
They tell us what the angels say.
Behold an infant pure and sweet –
Oh, come and worship at His feet.
See where Jesus rests his head,
See a humble manger bed,
Oh, hear the bells on Christmas ring –
The heav'nly hosts their praises sing!
Oh, hear the bells ring out with joy,

They tell us of an infant Boy.
Behold our King in stable bare –
Oh, come adore the Baby fair.
See the Savior of us all
Sleeping in a lowly stall,
Oh, hear the bells on Christmas ring –
What joyous news to men they bring!
Sancie Earman King

#

Christmas Day

Long ago and far away,
A tiny Child was born ...
To Joseph and to Mary
In stable so forlorn,
A King, He was without a throne
Or castle, rising high
In truth He was the Son of God!
Born, so He could die.
In raiment made of swaddling clothes,
He slept upon the hay.
Purer than the fresh-fallen snow ...
God's Son, in beauty lay.
The shepherds were the first to come,
To see and then believe
The words that had been told to them
That first Christmas Eve.
Through the centuries, come and gone,

His love shines ever true.
We change as we draw near to Him,
For He makes all things new.
Margaret Peterson

December 26

The Water of Life

Belief in Christ can quench our spiritual thirst, Canon R. C. Stephens assures us

Water is the most valuable substance in the world, for without it we could not exist and nothing would grow. Yet, because it is so easy to use by turning on a tap, many use it wastefully, forgetting that less than one hundred years ago people were drawing water from a well each day.

The people of Palestine in our Lord's time had a much more serious attitude towards water. They knew that life depended on a supply of it, and this is emphasized by the fact that water is mentioned in all but five of the books of the Old Testament. They never forgot that God had provided water for their forefathers during their wanderings in the desert, and physical thirst reminded them of a deeper thirst and longing within themselves – a thirst for God. As the psalmist said, "My soul is athirst for God, for the living God" (*Psalm 42:2*).

When we look at the New Testament, we find Jesus taking up the theme of spiritual thirst with the woman of Samaria at the well of Sychar, asking her for a drink. The woman argued, and He told her that He could give her living water "springing up into everlasting life" (*John 14:4*), but she did not understand

and could only think of the daily chore of fetching water; the spiritual meaning was lost on her.

On another occasion Jesus stood in the temple and cried, "If any man thirst, let him come unto me and drink, as the scripture hath said, out of the belly shall flow rivers of living water" (*John 7: 37,38*). Water only remains living water when it flows; when it ceases to flow it becomes stagnant.

Belief in Christ quenches our thirst; life becomes new and has a brightness and richness unknown before, but there are some today who find little point or purpose in living – they drift through life unhappy and lonely. If they would cleanse and satisfy them and they would have a compelling desire to share with others their joy, passing on the Good News of the Gospel.

December 27

Psalm 23

The Lord is my Shepherd; I shall not want. He maketh me to lie down in green pastures; he leadeth me beside still waters. He restoreth my soul; He leadeth me in the paths of righteousness for His name's sake.

Yea, though I walk through the valley of the shadow of death, I will fear no evil; for thou art with me; Thy rod and Thy staff they comfort me in the presence of mine enemies; Thou anointest my head with oil, my cup runneth over.

Surely goodness and mercy shall follow me all the days of my life; and I will dwell in the house of the Lord forever.

December 28

Be satisfied

Be satisfied with what you have,
Thank God for what is yours,
The Lord walks close beside you,
As long as time endures.
The bitter disappointments,
He will gently brush away,
His loving arms will hold you close,
Forever and a day.
You need not ever worry
That He will not understand,
Or that He'll push you from Him,
With a cold and careless hand.
For He knows our deepest longings,
And the tears we try to hide,
And His love is deep and lasting
And His arms are open wide.
Be satisfied though you may walk
The narrow way alone,
God's love for you does far surpass
All human love you've known.
You must believe that you are very
Special in His sight.
And trust He will not ever let
You stray from what is right.
In spite of all you may desire,
The dear Lord knows what's best
And through our weakest moments,
He helps us pass the test.

"To err is only human,
But to forgive, divine" ...
And in God's heart, forgiveness,
... is exactly what we find.
Grace E. Easley

December 29

A New Year's Prayer for You

There's always something special
about a brand new year.
It fills the heart with hope and joy
and prayerful, Godly cheer.
And as this year would crest its wake
we've made this prayer for you
That God would grant you much success
in all the good you do.
We ask He guard your health as well
and bring peace to your mind
To comfort you in all you face
in best and worst of times.
No matter what this year may bring
we pray Him you be near
For in Him we all overcome
and best our darkest fear.
And as you go from day to day
We pray with all our heart
that you reflect the love and grace
His precious Son imparts.
So Happy New Year, all of you,

this prayer is made for you
May God above prosper you all
with blessings old and new.

December 30 *

Never Look Back

Never look back on the past with regret
For the days that might have been,
Nor the promises made that were never kept
And the goals you did not win.
For life cannot always be perfect
And our days don't always shine bright,
And promises are sometimes broken
And dreams may not turn out just right.
But no time has ever been wasted
Nor did idle tears just fall
That the dear Lord was not watching
And understood it all.
For to everything there is a season,
A time to reap and a time to sow,
A time to laugh and a time to cry,
And a time for us to grow.
So, let the ghosts of past memories
Fade and slip away
For the promise of another season
Begins with another new day.
Jean V. Russell

December 31

The Best is Yet to Be

The New Year is a time for hope and promise, says Canon R. C. Stephens, when we are reminded of our future life in the kingdom of Heaven

Do we realize the part that anticipation plays in our lives and how dull they would be without it? We look forward to weddings, family outings and reunions, holidays, the birth of a child – the list is endless, and this spirit of expectancy contributes a great deal to our earthly happiness. I was therefore particularly shocked when a friend, about to retire, expressed his fear of being bored because there would be nothing to look forward to. Many people, finding themselves with nothing much to do after a busy working life, have had to embark on a period of readjustment and training for the days ahead.

As ordinary life is sustained by plans for the future, so also is the Christian life, for if our belief in Christ is limited to this world then "we of all men are most to be pitied" (*1 Corinthians 15:19*). It is not a matter of trying to be optimistic or putting on a brave face, but a matter of fact that God is good and in control, and joy comes from the promise of what is to be.

It is true that Jesus taught us to live a day at a time but He also directed attention to the future. He spoke of the kingdom which was to come, and told His friends that He went to prepare a place for them, emphasizing the reality of life in the hereafter.

Unfortunately, some dwell too much on past failures, which blur all thoughts of the future. St. Paul might have done the same, for his past could have weighed down his spirit but, trusting in Christ, he put all this behind him and pressed on "for the prize of the high calling of God" (*Philippians 3:14*).

The glory of the Christian faith is that "the best is yet to be", so at the beginning of a New Year, let us follow the Apostle's example and earnestly look forward with a hope which is inspired by God.

Biography

Jane Raphael Snowden was born June 26, 1922 and died at 88, in 2010, a widow for 15 years. My mother happily gambled her life on my dad and left her hometown of Kamloops, BC, Canada at the end of WWII for New York City, where my dad was employed. She was the only member of her five sibling family to venture away.

My mother and father had only one date before he shipped to the South Pacific in the US Navy. He had an Irish relative shipping out as well, who was raised in Kamloops so they spent their last days mainland. On a blind date with someone else the first night he got there, my dad approached my mom for a final date and that was it. While stationed on the Islands, my father asked my mother to marry him. She answered, "No." She couldn't commit to a man who may never come home as so many fellow Canadians had since entering the war in 1939. They married in October, 1944.

It was only what mom and dad said, while we were raised on Long Island. We went to church on Sundays. Rae, as she was always known, was a homemaker until we were into high school and college. She worked as an honest bookkeeper until it was time to retire with dad in Venice, Florida.

We were blessed with a good mom. Although, I know I often didn't see it that way. Mom was consistent in her upbringing. She gave us a set of morals that she lived by as well. She genuinely wanted to release us to live our own lives, never because of lack of love, or inconvenience. We were always welcome. She simply believed that life was meant to live and build a family that is ours. She tried her best to steer us, but let us go with our own choices and be prepared to accept what comes our way.

Mom and dad attended church and enjoyed retirement until my father died in 1996. I don't think it was too long after that when mom went on to put her life's work together. She pulled out her pile of clips and started matching dates to messages. The result was an inspiring book of mostly un-heard of common folk, but there are a number of great minds as well. Each one, I estimate to have been published 25 years ago or more. But, it seems like they were written yesterday.

Mom's was the true Christian journey, trying to manage life one day at a time under God's guidance. For her byline, I chose Rae Snowden Martin, and she was well-pleased. It used the name she was always known as, Rae, her cherished Canadian birth name, Snowden, and her proud American, Martin family name.

All of us children were at her bedside for her final days. Within two weeks of her death, the last page of her book that I read to her was Nov 5th, *"Death is but a bend in the road, not the end of the road."* She could barely be heard saying, "I use that line in my sympathy cards." I do it now as well.

She was not worried one bit about death. The Bible was enough for her to move on to Heaven. Her husband of over 50 years was waiting to greet her. When she made her last call to her little sister in Kamloops she declared, "I'm going to the OK Corral." With *"One Day at a Time, Lord,"* I'll never have to go further than my nightstand to chat with her on any day. If you are comforted by this book, please pass it along to someone else for their journey with the Lord, one day at a time.

Billy Martin

Rae Snowden Martin

Final Thoughts

The Man in the Glass

When you get what you want in the struggle for self
And the world makes you king for a day,
Just go to a mirror and look at yourself
And see what THAT man has to say.
For it isn't your father or mother or wife
Whose judgement upon you must pass
The fellow whose verdict counts most in your life
Is the one staring back from the glass.
Some people may think you a straight-shootin' chum
And call you a wonderful guy,
But the man in the glass says you're only a bum
If you can't look him straight in the eye.
He's the fellow to please, never mind all the rest,
For he's with you clear up to the end,
And you've passed your most dangerous, difficult test
If the man in the glass is your friend.
You may fool the whole world down the pathway of life
And get pats on the back as you pass,
But your final reward will be heartaches and fears
If you've cheated the man in the glass.

300

CPSIA information can be obtained
at www.ICGtesting.com
Printed in the USA
FSHW010536030221
78125FS